# Growing Up

## Biblical Youth Ministry in the Local Church

Dave Fenton

17 16 15 14 13 12 11 7 6 5 4 3 2 1

First published 2011 by Keswick Ministries and
Authentic Media Limited
Presley Way, Crownhill, Milton Keynes, MK8 0ES
www.authenticmedia.co.uk



**British Library Cataloguing in Publication Data**

A catalogue record for this book is available from the British Library

ISBN 978-1-85078-807-2



Cover design by David Smart
Printed and Bound in Great Britain by Cox and Wyman, Reading

# Contents

**Broader Issues**



**Epilogue**



**Appendices**

# Acknowledgements

I would like to place on record my thanks to the patient crowd at Authentic Media for their support of this book and their longing to see it in print. Particularly to Ali, Elizabeth and Sheila who made editorial comments on both structure and content.

Heidi Robinson (one of the youth leaders at my own church) did the line drawings that adorn the start of each chapter for which I am very grateful.

I have worked in many 'youth' contexts over the years and I am grateful to every one of the youth leaders I have worked with. They have been a stimulus and even, at times, a challenge but they have enriched my life with their own unique contributions. Youth teams at Belmont Chapel and Christ Church Fulwood were so supportive and gave time and energy very sacrificially. The list is too long to record but each one of them was valued. Thanks to Philip Hacking for creating the environment in which I flourished. Thanks to David Williams and the staff at Christ Church Winchester who gave me every encouragement to keep going and finish the book. Particularly to the Butterworth family who asked me most weeks how the writing was going.

Mostly to my wonderful family who are such an inspiration to me. My three children, their wonderful wives and my seven grandchildren, remind me daily of God's goodness. But chiefly to my wonderful wife, Heather, who gave up several holidays and had me glued to my lap top and kept coffee and wine gums appearing on my table. She also read the whole thing a few times and corrected some grammatical errors. She truly deserves the praise for her faithfulness.

I am most grateful to the living God who saved me through the blood of his son and gave me a hope and a future to pass on to young people. To him be all the glory.

# Preface

For over one hundred and thirty years, the Keswick Convention has played a vital role in the growth of the worldwide evangelical faith. However, while there are millions of Christians who honour the name of Keswick, many have limited knowledge of the Convention's core values and commitments. This new series attempts to address that gap in understanding.

By providing key studies into some of the major emphases of the Convention, the prayer of its Trustees is that a new generation will be inspired afresh, in the words of Keswick's motto, to be 'All one in Christ Jesus'. And since the 'All' includes all types and ages, it is highly appropriate to incorporate a volume on biblical youth ministry in this series. Many of us as parents, grandparents and members of local churches are painfully aware of the gap that so often exists between young and old both in society and the church. How can we address that? How is a rising generation going to hear and learn of Jesus?

Over the many decades of Keswick, countless young lives, many of them students, have been challenged and changed by the Spirit of God revealing Jesus through his Word. Presently, however, many of us are aware of our need for regular encouragement and practical 'how to' help in pressing on in the joyful but so often hard work of winning younger hearts and minds for Christ. Thankfully Dave Fenton, who for many years has exercised a most fruitful ministry amongst young people both in a local church setting and at the Keswick Convention itself, has provided *Growing Up*. Here you will find both inspiration and practical help from the hand of a seasoned encourager and practitioner.

Welcome to a much anticipated addition to the Keswick Foundations series.

*Steve Brady*
*Moorlands College*
*Series Editor*

# Introduction:

# We All Started Somewhere

A sunny day on a beach in South Devon – the sea was sparkling, and my future wife and I were taken out for a cream tea overlooking the water. It certainly gave me good reason to consider ministry in that part of the world. I was finishing my training as a teacher, and we were going to be married in the summer and take on two new jobs. The donor of the tea was the youth leader at Belmont Chapel (a large Brethren assembly in Exeter, my wife's home town and church). He was a larger than life figure; a man of immense energy with a vision to match. Under his leadership the youth ministry had flourished. We were his latest recruits; Bernard did his recruiting in style and had the ability to cast a vision that exuded a passion for gospel ministry. We all need both a sense of calling to youth ministry and a vision of what God has for us to do, and we were certainly made aware of Bernard's vision that day. It made me want to be part of growing God's kingdom, but it also made me want to work with this man who had given us a great afternoon out.

Over the cream tea, and with all the passion of a man committed to his young people, we were told about the long-term vision of the youth ministry and the crucial part we would play in this expanding work. There were young people in Exeter who were lost without Jesus, we were informed, and we must reach them with the gospel. His awareness of what it means to be 'lost' was something that made a deep impression on me.

He had realized that youth ministry needed a core of Bible teaching earthed in the reality of young people's lives and, although he wasn't the 'coolest' leader I've ever met, any young person in his care knew two things. Firstly, Bernard loved his Lord and he relished any opportunity to speak about Jesus. We used to ask him if he ever stopped talking about the man from Nazareth! Secondly, he had a deep concern for the young people in his care; he knew about their lives and shared in their experiences.

Bernard's ministry was built on two key principles: 'preach the word' (2 Tim. 4:2) and 'Care for the flock' (1 Pet. 5:2, NLT). Close to the end of his forty-two years on earth, many asked why God had taken him so prematurely, and why God didn't leave the good guys on the planet and take the bad guys out of circulation. Just weeks before his death we were running a young people's camp in Dorset. He could do little more than sit on a camp bed and watch what was happening. Much of his worldly strength had ebbed away, but he called me over and said that he knew the future of youth ministry in Belmont Chapel was in safe hands – *mine*! At his thanksgiving service, the preacher took Joshua 1 as his text and said, 'Moses my servant is dead, now Joshua arise' (see Josh. 1:2).

I didn't hear much more – I had heard what God wanted me to hear that day and I knew that my life was to be dedicated to youth ministry. That thanksgiving service was clear confirmation that I was called to leadership in youth ministry, although I didn't enter into full-time service for some years after that. I had served my apprenticeship under this man's leadership and I cannot overstate the effect that Bernard had on my life. In my early years as youth leader at Belmont Chapel, I often asked myself the question 'What would Bernard do here?' Whether this was due to my insecurity or the knowledge that this man was full of integrity and wisdom I'm not sure, but I would certainly come up with a good answer.

There were others who came after Bernard. We moved to Sheffield and I became a senior teacher in a large comprehensive school. We attended Christ Church Fulwood, a large evangelical Anglican church on the western fringe of Sheffield. For five years I led a school mathematics department, but with a growing conviction that I was being called to full-time ministry. That school taught me a lot about the leadership of a team and using people's gifts in creative ways. It also gave me a much broader insight than leafy Exeter into the kind of young people who live in both middle-class suburbs and those who live in the inner city. This was very much an action-packed five years, as I found a culture very different to the one I had experienced in the south-west of England.

In my time there, youth unemployment became a real issue, as the industrial base of Sheffield life was collapsing, and the dozens of apprentices we sent to the steelworks dwindled each year. The pattern of school life followed automatically by immediate employment was never to return.

It became clear to me that what was being taught in secondary education was not wholly based on a Christian world-view. Life was about *you* and *your* career, about *your* future and achieving *your* potential. These aims were very laudable but would not develop the complete individual. The concepts of service and spirituality were hardly addressed in the curriculum. It was also apparent that many children found the atmosphere of an urban comprehensive school a threatening one and, realistically, did not fulfil the comprehensive dream of the integration of students of whatever ability. Those in top sets generally came from the upper part of the catchment area, and lower abilities came from the lower part. They rarely met, and the hopes and aspirations of those groups of children were very different. We had a huge range of socio-economic groups in that school and, as I dealt with all of them, it was obvious that a wide range of pastoral and communication skills were needed. I realized that gospel ministry would be very different depending on the area.

After I had worked for five years in a Sheffield school, Christ Church Fulwood began the search for a new youth worker. I was asked to write the job description and be part of the interviewing panel. One candidate returned for a second day of interviews, but we realized he was not the man for the job. Close to the end of that day, those who had shared the interview panel with me gathered around me and asked if I would consider the role. I had, apparently, been asking all the right questions! They saw that I had a vision and a passion for the work, and could see that I had ways to implement that vision. This would involve a change of career, a severe drop in salary and a sacrificial act by Heather, my wife, to fund our family with her teaching skills. Our world was changing; I had entered the world of so-called full-time ministry. Every Christian believer should see themselves as being in 'full-time ministry', but it seems to be the label of convenience for those of us called to serve the church in a salaried role. It was here that I met another man who profoundly influenced my life. Philip Hacking had been the vicar of the parish for some years, and built up the congregation from very small beginnings to a church roll of over a thousand. It was no surprise to me when I discovered the 'secret' of his fruitfulness in ministry. He had preached the word faithfully even though he was committed to many national initiatives (the Keswick Convention being a significant one), but he knew his own patch and cared for his congregation. Christ Church was an exciting place to be part of, and in many ways it was a repeat run of what I had seen in the voluntary ministry which I had been part of in Belmont Chapel.

Early on, I found the role quite frustrating as I could so easily become distracted. I missed the camaraderie of the school staff room, where teachers would gather and drink endless cups of coffee every lunch and break time. As a church youth minister you are likely to be the only specialist and, even though you are part of a staff team, other team members have different priorities. I had to invent schedules for myself and, although I am not the most structured person in the world, some time management was crucial. I used to set aside days or half days where I would do routine administration, and some where I worked on long-term planning – a day to plan the summer house party, or a day for study and reflection (I wasn't good at those!). Slowly but surely I adapted to the new rhythm of life and the fact that I had to be self-motivating and decide priorities – nobody else was going to do that for me!

Over the years I have reflected on what style of leadership encourages good youth ministry. My best shot at a descriptive phrase is 'permissive encouragement'. I flourished because there was a freedom to bring young people into all aspects of church life and to try to work within the whole church context. There were no battles to get young people involved. Philip's obvious support and encouragement, coupled with a clear investment of finance and buildings for the work, meant that youth ministry was high profile and often mentioned in the pulpit and in church committees as being a key activity in the life of the church. (Some later chapters will deal with aspects of church life which are crucial to the nurture of young disciples.)

There have been many more who have made an impact on my life and helped me to do things better. I remain convinced that church should be a place of security and challenge for young people – a 'safe' place for them to grow as disciples of Christ. There have been moments of pain and frustration when people have not shared my vision and passion, and there will always be people who oppose your plans – and, even worse, will be opposed to you. It's then that you cling to your calling and the sense of purpose that God has given you.

It is good to look back and give thanks to God for the people who have shaped our lives and given us the motivation to press on in ministry. If we fail to understand the way people have influenced us, we will never understand what makes us tick.

**THINK AND ACT**

Think about a couple of people who have impacted your life and ministry.

- Give thanks for them.
- List the ways in which they impacted you.
- If you can contact them and thank them, then do it.

Much of what I share in this book is the result of the influence of godly men and women who have given something of themselves to me. In the years I have been involved with youth ministry in the local church and at national level, I have encountered many versions of so-called youth ministry. I have met many practitioners and been involved with several churches in shaping their work in this area. The statistics are not good – the church is not keeping a lot of its young people. My passion is to see groups of young people engaged with their leaders in living for Christ and becoming more mature in their faith. We are not just a holding action – we must not think that we are just hanging on to young people until they are ready to join an adult congregation. That lacks any kind of positive agenda in response to what God has commanded us to do. But, if we are not sure what we are trying to do and we are meeting only because we think we ought to be doing something, we will not have groups which will flourish.

I have met many willing people who want to be effective as youth ministers, but they freely admit they are not quite sure how to go about it. This book is designed to lay down some biblical principles upon which to build your work, and some guidance about how to make it work in practice. Youth ministry will have its joys and moments of sadness but, if we're not sure what we're doing, those 'lows' will be much harder to cope with. If we have some clarity about what we are trying to do, we have a purpose which will help us through the pressures we face. I love the poster I once saw outside a church: 'What on earth are you doing for heaven's sake?' I hope this book will give some building blocks for your ministry, but will also help you continue to build on those sure foundations.

In my present post at Christ Church Winchester, it is a real joy to see youth ministry being given its proper place by the way it is both resourced and encouraged. Young people are growing and becoming involved in all kinds of service outlets. I long to find more churches which not only have a passion to minister to young people, but put resources and people in place to make it happen.

As Charles Wesley allegedly once said: 'If religion is not extended to the children, what will be the outcome?'[1]

# FOUNDATIONS

# 1.

# The World of Youth Ministry

## A familiar story

Jane is a mum in her late thirties. She is committed to serving the children at her church as is her husband Peter, who is an elder – he used to run the Pathfinder group. Their Sunday routine has never been broken since the day they were married. If there was something that needed doing at church, they often filled in the gap; they were a well-known and much-loved family. Their three children had always gone to church with them every Sunday morning, progressing through the children's groups and into the youth group. They had always seemed keen to know about God and to be involved in the life of their groups and the wider church community.

But two weeks earlier their eldest son, John, had come home from school with, what he thought, was a very innocent request. He wanted to run in the school cross-country team because he had been performing very well in practice. The event was to be held on a Sunday morning. Jane and Peter were unsure how they should respond. Should they give church a miss and go to support their son? Would this be the beginning of John's loss of faith? It was only for one Sunday, but would more events crop up in the future? Were they making a big issue out of something that just had to be dealt with? Perhaps they knew that as many as 2,000 people a week have been leaving our churches in England over the past decade, and half of those were under 15. Would their precious son be another 'leaving church' statistic? After all, children have to start making their own decisions at some point. When should they give them a free choice – if ever?

## Stay alert

Many Christian parents and church leaders have grappled with this scenario. The decline in church attendance is well documented and can make pretty depressing reading. Peter Brierley, in his book *Pulling Out of the Nose Dive*,[1] gives us some interesting data (added bullet points mine)

- . . . There was a huge decline in numbers of young people in the 1990s, when over that decade some 500,000 stopped going to church
- Not only are we struggling to keep and care for young people from church families, we are making negligible impact on the vast majority of young people who are un-churched

But we should be encouraged by another statement in his book

- The catastrophic drop among those under 15 in the 1990s has slowed considerably to a much smaller annual rate of loss between 1998 and 2005
- There has been a decreasing decline in numbers of those aged 15 to 19 leaving the church. Perhaps those who 'make it' through the crisis years of 11 to 14 are more inclined to stay.

However, we must record four stark facts

- Not every church has young people in its congregation
- 39 per cent of churches had no one attending under 11 years of age
- 49 per cent of churches had no one attending between 11 and 14
- 59 per cent of churches had no one attending between 15 and 19 years of age

This means that if you turn up to your local church with no other criteria in mind other than 'it's local' you have about a 50 per cent chance of finding any provision for the 11 to 18s. The steady decline of young people within the church remains. When this decline was first noted, many of the counter initiatives were started at the para-church level. Very little thinking was being done by the local church to see what was needed to be more effective in youth ministry. I want to examine the key principles and the good practice that will revive effective ministry at the local church level. In the UK we are generally quite good at Sunday school work but, as I often say to incredulous youth leaders on training courses, a 9-year-old will be 10 years old next year and 11 years old the year after that and so on. So, if you have an excellent crèche and Sunday school and no provision for 11 plus in your church, you are setting up the perfect scenario for children to fall off the edge of church life. That has a rather irresponsible feel.

## Basic motivation

All the churches I have visited have stories of young people who have drifted away from meeting with Christians, just as there are stories of adults who lose their faith and wander off. But the problem is particularly acute in the younger teenagers. Many churches seem to have a kind of cling-on mentality – the Klingons were wicked beings in *Star Trek* and just clinging on to young people is not a helpful model of ministry. If we regard our work as simply hanging on at all costs, we will appear to be negative and may do unhelpful things. We may try simply to entertain them just to keep them happy, but do very little to shape their lives and to help them grow as mature believers in Jesus Christ. We must never think of youth ministry as a holding action until the day of great relief when they finally make it to adulthood, and then they'll all be fine. Young people in the age range from 11 to 18 are in a time of their life in which ideas are shaped, world-views are formed and morals established; it is a period when they are searching for a faith that is true and works in their world. At this time of great opportunity we have the privilege of helping them find truth and reality in the person of Jesus. We have to believe that, and make it a priority of the local church community.

**THINK AND ACT**

What do you see as the main driver of youth ministry in your church?

- Maintenance of the group
- Entertainment
- Keeping parents happy
- Making mature disciples
- Something else

Take a look at your programme.

- What does it say about your priorities?

In staffing terms, we often find churches who struggle to get people to volunteer whether there is a full-time worker in the church or not. Most churches of any size will have leadership teams with a mixture of paid pastors and volunteers spending a lot of work and committee time on the maintenance of the church. Buildings and finance often are the key elements of any agenda. All this has to be done but, as children grow into young people, they need people who will do the 1 Thessalonians thing

> But we were gentle among you, like a nursing mother taking care of her own children. . . . we were ready to share with you not only the gospel of God but also our own selves, because you had become very dear to us. (1 Thess. 2:7,8)

We need people who will share their lives, share the gospel, and love young people with a full, open and generous heart. In simple terms, we need people who love the Lord and love to minister in his name. Sadly, volunteers are often dragooned into service, not trained, and expected to live out a life sentence in Sunday school or youth ministry with little support. Everyone is happy for Jane and her family to turn up week after week and run the crèche, but nobody asks her how she's doing and whether she needs help. Maybe she needs a couple of weeks off so she can go to watch her son run a cross-country race, without feeling guilty.

## Biblical roots

If you look at Psalm 78, Asaph tells us some of the great things God has done for his people, the Israelites. We hear about the law being established in Israel (v. 5), about the parting of the Red Sea which enabled the people to escape the butchery of Pharaoh's chariots, and we also hear, in many verses, about the way God's people drifted away from the purpose God had for them. Sound familiar? The great deeds of a great God are meshed in with the behaviour of a disobedient people. That is why the psalm starts as it does, to remind the people of the 'glorious deeds of the LORD, and his might, and the wonders that he has done', and we must not 'hide them from [our] children, but tell to the coming generation' (Ps. 78:4). If we know the God who has done the glorious things Asaph records, then the psalm makes clear that we have no alternative but to tell them to the next generation, and a failure to do so will have serious consequences. We have to tell our children and the generation after that. By so doing, we generate a tradition (some traditions are good!) that we cannot allow any following generation to remain ignorant about God. If they don't hear about God they will not 'set their hope in God', they will forget the works of God and will not 'keep his commandments' (v. 7). If we break the generation chain Asaph speaks of, then there will be future generations who know nothing of God; they will become a 'stubborn and rebellious generation' (v. 8) and the word of God's truth will be lost to many. Perhaps that is what is on Jane and Peter's mind as they drive to church with only two children in the back of their car, wondering how their eldest son is doing in the cross-country race. Will their precious son drift away from the church and become part of the stubborn generation, and will they join the ranks of the parents longing to see their children restored to Christian fellowship?

Faced with all the pressures of family life, parents need to know what their children are getting in church, but there is no biblical support for a babysitting service for children of any age. Families are responsible for the nurture of their children, but we are also encouraged to put that in a framework of biblical community. It should not be expected of parents that they bring up their children only within the family environment. Children have always been part of the community of faith. The leaders of the early church told people about Jesus and encouraged them to join a community of faith where they could grow. Paul's instruction to Timothy is

> So then you are no longer strangers and aliens, but you are fellow citizens with the saints and members of the household of God . . . In [Jesus] you also are being built together into a dwelling place for God by the Spirit'
>
> Ephesians 2:19–22

And I guess the longing in Peter and Jane's heart is that their son 'had such a mind as this always, to fear [him] and to keep all [his] commandments' (Deut. 5:29). They will have striven, as so many parents have, to bring up their son to know and follow the Lord, and their fear is that he is losing that desire as he is attracted by things, however wholesome, that will lead him away from faithful discipleship. Therefore the foundation of biblical youth ministry is to provide a place where the Word of God is taught and applied in ways that will challenge young people to live godly lives in a secular community. Our plan should be to see young men and women becoming more like Christ in all their ways (see Prov. 3:6). If a child belongs to a Christian home, then growth and nurture must happen there; but for everyone, the household of God, the church, must be a place where teaching leads to changed lives.

## Key elements

I believe there are four key elements of Christian youth ministry which should all be in place if we are to see our young people grow to maturity in our youth groups. We have to ask ourselves about what we need to do to minister to individuals who will be drawn away by counter attractions such as the cross-country team. But we must not allow ourselves to see our work as competing with the secular world. We can either complain about the modern Sunday or try to help our youth think 'Christianly' when they are in their twenty-first century world. As ministers to young people, we are doing something that no one else is doing for them. We are not another counter attraction because we are doing something that the living God has commanded us to do, and it is unique.

What should be the building blocks on which we establish Christian youth ministry in the local church? We should try to build a community where young people can

- Become Christians
- Grow as Christians
- Live as Christians
- Serve as Christians

These four elements in youth ministry are based on how the Bible defines the life of a believer. If we look at the book of Acts, we see a church determined to proclaim the gospel so that people might believe and *become Christians*. We see Paul writing to many churches who were experiencing problems with the *growth* of their believers, and he gives them help as to how that should be done: 'never . . . put a stumbling block or hindrance in the way of a brother' (Rom. 14:13).

Clearly they were getting it wrong and needed help with growing as mature Christians.

To live in today's young world is not easy. It is simply not good enough for us to say to young people 'Go out into your world and witness to your faith!' without helping them to see how that can be done. It's a hostile world; let's be honest, how many adult Christians do that anyway? Perhaps the bit we miss out most is involving young people in service ministries in our church because we regard them as adults waiting to happen. We are reluctant to let them loose in services or in other 'adult only' areas, and this only serves to make them feel they don't belong; so they leave, disillusioned. Nobody is suggesting that the church should only serve the under-18s but perhaps the bias needs correcting.

**THINK AND ACT**

- How much of your youth ministry time is spent in each of the four areas?
- Why do you think that happens?
- What do you need to put in place to correct your bias?
- How does your church deal with youth ministry? Do adults know what's going on? Is it valued by your church?

There is a chapter (or part of one) devoted to each of these four key elements where ideas will be developed. We must build our ministries on something like these points which will guide and direct our programme. If you aim at nothing, you'll probably hit nothing! There has to be intentionality in what we do.

As a parent of three children, I wanted to know that my children were not just being entertained or 'clung on to', but that they were being challenged to be young men who wanted to please God in the multiplicity of activities and pastimes in which they were involved. Jane and Peter's son may well have been taught this way, in which case his leaders would have been able to talk with and pray for him as good pastor-teachers of their flock – as well as giving his parents love and support as their son began to ask the questions most teenagers ask.

If youth ministry is to be effective, it must be seen as a key activity in the life of the church. All ages in the church community need to be committed to it if it is to flourish. Jane and Peter need to be supported and released from guilt in the decisions they make about their children. The whole church needs to own, support and pray for those who are in the work. As I watch our children leave for their groups on Sundays, I am profoundly grateful for every single one of them. They are part of our community and need to be acknowledged as such. Youth ministry comes to grief when it is regarded as a babysitting operation, and people such as Jane are regarded as 'keeping the kids occupied' so we can have a 'proper service without noisy disturbance'. Jane and Peter are key people – youth ministry has biblical foundations and they are fulfilling God's command. Let's start a rethink (if we need to) about the purpose of our children's and youth ministry and how we can make it prosper for the sake of the kingdom.

## Books

Ken Moser et al, *No Guts, No Glory* (London: St Matthias Press, 2000).

Mark Ashton, Phil Moon, Jonathan Carswell, *Christian Youth Work – A Strategy for the Local Church* (Milton Keynes: Authentic Media, 2007).

# 2.

# Faithful Servants

George Burton was the leader of the Mayflower Centre in the sixties. He operated in the east end of London and made the centre a place for young people because they had little else to do. He wrote a book about his experiences, *People Matter More Than Things*.[1] Whether we are parents, church leaders or youth ministers we need to appreciate the people who serve in youth and children's ministry. These people are the salt of the earth because they are the people who make it happen. We undervalue them at our peril.

The reason young people come to youth group is quite simply the people – their mates and their leaders. Those wonderful leaders have often done a hard day's work, got their family to bed and completed something for the office before they come along. In my own church we have a person who daily commutes over one hundred miles, works as a manager in a pressure sales environment, comes home to his wife and three children, but is always there on a Sunday morning with his small group. These people are heroes and should be treated as such because if our aim is to teach God's Word to God's young people, we need those gifted to do it. This is another foundation of good youth ministry; whether that's two leaders (you need a minimum of two to cover both genders) operating with six young people, or twenty leaders serving 100 young people, the principles of leadership are the same.

Almost every church I have visited which is engaged in youth ministry is short of staff. Many volunteers find it hard to maintain a weekly commitment – their world is just too busy. Youth ministry demands a high level of relational skill if it is to function well, and many find that hard to keep going. Is there an ideal profile of the person most suited to youth ministry? Is it the coolest person in the church, and do they have to be under 23, otherwise there is no chance they can connect with young people?

In recent years, many larger churches have appointed full- or part-time workers to minister to young people. There are now about seven thousand people employed by UK churches to do youth, or youth and children's ministry. Does this solve all the problems? It can cause volunteers to melt into the background, so care needs to be taken in pulling together the work of the staff member and the volunteers. I know that getting people involved in this ministry is costly for them, but it is vital if the youth are going to meet leaders who are committed followers of Jesus, who love his Word and have a passion to see young people mature in Christ. So we must do anything we can to make their lives as easy as possible, and give them good training to equip them for the task.

## What is the ideal?

What should we be looking for in the appointment of either a volunteer or a full-time worker? In any other area of ministry in the church we look for people who have the spiritual gift to fulfil that role – we also need to consider their availability. There is the temptation to look only for the person who is culturally accessible to the youth group. That will often lead us to people very close to the age of the group. These people will lack experience and can be quite immature Christians who will not be able to offer all the wisdom young people require. Young leaders are vital to youth ministry, but they are not the sum total of what we need. Our culture suggests that to be young is everything, and the younger you are the more effective you are likely to be. I have met youth leaders who should have retired at 25 or earlier, and I know of people in their sixties who are a magnet for young people. The reason is obvious. If the 23-year-old is not gifted but very capable of fruitful service in another ministry, that's where they should be; and if the 60-year-old has both the gifting and the passion to work with young people, keep them going as long as they are effective! One hears some ageist arguments put forward in this area but if the post-60 person is still an effective teacher and/or disciple maker, why should they stop? If our primary focus is to be effective pastor/teachers, then please let's use people who have the gift.

In my visit to Australia in 1999, I was struck by the kind of leaders who were training young people in discipleship. There were plenty of 'young bucks' around the conference, but the teachers and small group leaders were mature believers (one in his seventies) who were deeply respected by the young people. Each group had a younger assistant leader who was still learning from their group leader, and I didn't see many group leaders running around the sports field. Their role as a teacher was honoured by the young people. Perhaps the prevailing youth culture has eaten away too many crucial values in this area.

**THINK AND ACT**

Think about the current age profile of the team in your church.

- Try to identify the gifts and strengths of each person on your current team.
- Take a look at your church roll – highlight the names of possible new team members on the basis of their spiritual maturity, not their cultural appeal.
- Make a list of those people and begin praying for each of them.
- Try to arrange an informal meeting with the one who you would most like to have on your team.
- Keep praying about the other name(s).

My 'dream team' (which I have rarely achieved) would contain gifted people from a whole range of backgrounds. Looking at the profiles and gifting of our teams is a useful exercise because it gives us something more defined to pray for, rather than just asking God for more workers. I once prayed for someone to deal with all the resourcing of our work with pens, papers and so on. I ended up with a retired headmistress who used to get a taxi to the city stationery store and would regularly nag us with, 'If you don't tell me what you need, how on earth can I get it for you?' She encouraged me to look beyond the traditional areas one would usually recruit from. Catering was my living nightmare, and I found people who were happy to dish up food at any time of the day or night. One woman led a team of cooks on our summer house parties, and was much loved as a brilliant chef and as a woman whose service was carried out with a lovely servant spirit. The young people saw servant ministry in the kitchen as well as in the teaching sessions.

There are some people who love doing repair jobs around the church, and I even knew someone once who took real pride in putting chairs in neat rows. Not everyone is gifted in teaching ministry, but these other giftings are invaluable because they release the teachers and small group leaders to do what they're gifted to do. We had a retired man who was a DIY fanatic and would love nothing better than to come into the building and repair anything that was broken. We never had table tennis bats with flappy rubber faces, or snooker cues with no tips – he saw to that.

In the ministry team I would try to recruit as balanced a group as I could manage. There might be a married couple with children who could only give limited time, but I would also want some singles to be on the team. A bright university student would be great, but I would also want somebody who entered the world of work at 16 or 18. Balance is very helpful because young people need to see that the Christian walk works whether you're 25 or 65.

You will rarely recruit someone who ticks all your boxes, but if you know where your gaps are it may well lead you to someone who has some of the gifts you need to make your group function well. Most of you are wondering at this point how you grab hold of somebody to double your own team strength to two, but as your team grows, look to maintain diversity; the major criteria is always their gifting to work with young people, as well as their genuine sense of calling to serve in this way.

The Bible gives us clear guidance about the qualities of Christian leadership, and I see no reason to look further than this in a search for youth leaders. Most of the qualities refer to character. 1 Timothy has a list in chapter 3. They should be

- Above reproach
- Husband of one wife
- Sober-minded
- Self-controlled
- Respectable
- Hospitable
- Able to teach
- Not a drunkard
- Not violent but gentle
- Not quarrelsome
- Not a lover of money
- Manage his own house well

. . . and so on.

Titus 1 has a similar list of qualities. Before we get to the point of establishing gifts, we need to know that we are talking to men and women of integrity. We recruit only people who have a true and genuine commitment to gospel ministry, otherwise we could well make a rod for our own back. It's only then we start to establish whether a person is someone who could make a contribution to the ministry.

## How do we recruit?

The clever answer to the question is 'with difficulty'. So many churches find it hard to recruit helpers and, once they've got them, keeping hold of them. The temptation is to jump on the first mildly attractive personality who appears to be unemployed in church life, and sentence them to thirty years work in a Pathfinder group with no remission. No wonder people give up. The way we deal with our volunteers in church life is crucial if we are to maintain a healthy ministry and a vibrant church. When I approached someone to help with our youth ministry I always tried to convey these ideas

1. This conversation is about seeking after God's will for your life – it is no shame to say after a time (or straight away) that youth ministry is not for you.
2. Let's talk about your gifts and how you could be used in our ministry. There will be times where everybody just mucks in to get the job done (clear up at the end of an evening), but we want you to exercise the spiritual gifts God has given you.
3. You need to go through a checking process both with the church leader and the Criminal Records Bureau, and your appointment is dependent on both.
4. Come along for a trial period.

Each of these is important – it makes your new recruit realize that you regard their appointment as a serious issue, and you care about their gifts and how they can be used. You are not simply grabbing them so you can dump all the tedious jobs on them. You are handling your most precious resource because these are the people who will do the job Psalm 78 demands. If we are to teach the Bible, we need people who are effective; we also need people who will create the environment for the Bible to be taught and where honest discussion can take place. At this stage, I am not looking for eminent theologians, but for teachable individuals who have a thirst to grow in their own understanding and share their God-given wisdom with young people. I am also looking for approachable people who will not repel youth, but rather those who love to sit down and talk with an open Bible, and search for truth within its pages. I'm also interested in people who have a measure of wisdom learned from living a life devoted to Jesus; this does not mean someone who appears to have lived a monastic existence, but rather a person who has been through life and known God's leading and guidance and his sustaining grace. That will be rare in a young leader; I want mature persons on the team who can help both the young people *and* mentor the younger leaders. Above all, I want those whose ambition is to be more Christ-like day by day, and who have learned that a sense of fun is not excluded from godliness.

## Make it clear

When a new leader arrives in the group they often find it quite difficult to get started, and want to give up after a few weeks. The other leaders all know the young people, they know the recent history, they know what's been fun and laughed about and they know what's been sad. The new leader knows nothing of all this so must be welcomed by the other leaders so that everyone knows who this person is and why they've joined the team. After that probationary call-seeking time, a decision must be made, and made clear to everybody. You are trying to create a team that will deliver your purpose of making mature disciples, and you need to be sure that your new recruit has the same goals. You need a person who is committed to the goals of the team.

Here are a few first steps in building your new recruit into the team.

1. It must be made clear to the new team member what your group is about – aims and values need to be documented, but not rigidly adhered to. Some leaders like to keep power in their own hands by refusing to document anything, so that they become the sole authority for the direction of the group.
2. New leaders can become frustrated when they don't have a clue what they should do and they don't have a clear role – after a few weeks, try to give them a minor role and see how they deal with it.
3. Make it absolutely clear what the real issues are for the group and what its purpose is. Talk to them about the emphasis on teaching and on how you regard the Bible as the authority in all matters of faith and conduct.
4. Appoint your new leader properly with a letter of appointment, whether that is a team of two or twenty. The letter should be signed by your church leader.
5. Make clear what your expectation is – when do the leaders meet, either with the young people or as a ministry team. Get some dates in the diary.

All of these things give the new leader (and the rest of the team) a real sense of worth and belonging. With modern communication, there is little excuse for not keeping your team informed about all aspects of the work.

## Who does what?

There are many roles to be covered in the life of most youth groups. There is food to be cooked and equipment to be maintained. We need teachers and someone to look after the pastoral needs, as well as enough people to run small groups. You soon learn who are gifted teachers and who are the gifted administrators (that is a spiritual gift – 1 Cor. 12:28), and leaders need clarity about their place in the youth ministry set-up. So many groups effectively say 'just turn up and see what needs doing' and nobody seems to quite know when you do get there. Always remember that the people who 'just turn up each week' are going to be those people who 'teach and admonish' (see Col. 1:28) the young people. These are those who will do the work of ministry, so we need to exercise care over who does it – and we need to care for them once they've started.

So now we know what youth ministry is about and we have a group of gospel ministers in place to do the work of ministry. If I have made these steps sound really easy, you must forgive me because I know how hard this is to achieve. It took me many years to get anywhere near this model! When I went to see the youth ministry at Willow Creek Community Church near Chicago, I met the leader. Bo Boshers was a man of great energy and passion – he never seemed to let up; it made me feel tired just to see him at work. But he taught me some good lessons and these are the ones I remember.

1. When you listen to me talk about youth ministry, don't think you can replicate it – you probably can't.
2. Have some principles which underpin your work and make sure everybody around knows what they are (you may not agree with all of mine, but make sure you know what you're trying to achieve). If you aim at nothing, you'll probably hit it.
3. Dream your dreams but do your job.[2]

To me the last one says everything about how I want to operate. Young people need leaders who will turn up week by week and faithfully serve God. However, those leaders should never lose sight of the aim of producing young people devoted to Jesus Christ. We also need leaders of vision who don't just work on a week-by-week basis, but can create and implement a vision as God leads them. Just think about your group of ten young people and imagine what happens when they go to university or into the workplace to speak of Jesus, to live for Jesus and serve Jesus. They join up with churches who use them to be youth leaders, or even Bible teachers. Some of them may get married and have children who grow up learning how to follow Jesus. In the nicest possible way, you don't have a clue what you're doing when you work with your group. I'm ancient enough to see both the joys and disappointments of youth ministry. Some do fall by the wayside and they're often the surprising ones, bearing in mind how keen they were in the group. But others don't fall away, and they fulfil helpful roles as adults. You are in the kingdom business to serve the King.

**THINK AND ACT**

Think about your own leadership team.

- How do you recruit them?
- How do you appoint them?
- How do you get them started?
- How do you tell them what's happening?
- Could you improve things, and how?

## Books

Tim Hawkins, *Leaders Who Will Last* (Surrey: The Good Book Company, 2002).

# 3.

# Culture: A Friend, an Enemy, or Neither?

When I was writing this chapter, Heather and I were staying in our caravan in Cornwall. One night we went out to eat and ended up taking home a Chinese meal. (I believe in giving my wife a good time!) The lady who served us asked who we were and what we were doing in Cornwall, and I said we had taken a few days away to try to get this book finished.

'What are you writing a book about?' she asked, then continued about her life history and all her recent contacts with the church. She said she found most churches a bit sombre, but when her husband was dying she had come across a hospital chaplain who was brilliant in the way he handled her situation. For her, somebody had penetrated into her world and made God relevant to the situation she was struggling with.

## Engaging with our world

Most people's perception is that the church does not connect because it simply fails to understand the modern world. Many non-churchgoers believe that Christians have barely made it into the twentieth century, let alone the twenty-first. We are perceived as living in a kind of fantasy world with an ageing population, and it won't be long before the church disappears. But we need not fear extinction because God has promised otherwise: 'they will perish but you remain . . . your years will have no end' (Heb. 1:11,12).

Our ability to make the gospel known is severely hampered by our failure and reluctance to try to understand the world we live in. My Chinese take-away lady wanted a place to go, but couldn't find one until someone engaged with her at her time of need. There will always be people who reject the gospel, however good the interaction has been, but perhaps we need to learn a lesson from the apostle Paul who, when faced with the intellectual might of Greece, had clearly done his homework

> So Paul, standing in the midst of the Areopagus, said:
> 'Men of Athens, I perceive that you are very religious.
> For as I passed along and observed the objects of your worship,
> I found also an altar with this inscription, "To the unknown god."
> What therefore you worship as unknown, this I proclaim to you.'
>
> (Acts 17:22,23)

Paul then goes on to talk of the God he knows and gets a mixed reaction: 'some mocked. But others said, "We will hear you again about this"' (Acts 17:32).

These verses tell us a great deal about our interaction with young people and the world they inhabit. Paul stood in the midst of the secular world of Hellenistic culture and was not afraid to comment about it because he had seen it for himself – he had seen the temples of Athens and all their brilliant architecture, reflecting human achievement. He had also seen a weakness in their panoply of gods which said that one of their gods was 'unknown'. That was an open door which Paul could not resist, and he talked at length about the God who could be known and experienced. In doing so, he challenged one of their fundamental beliefs that God was so far removed from earthly realties he could not possibly have come to earth to dirty himself by his suffering and death. This 'God in a body' concept was far removed from their understanding of their gods, and a very new and challenging doctrine. Some Athenians were clearly attracted by the idea because they 'believed' (Acts 17:34) – but not all of them.

Far from wallowing in their culture, Paul had engaged with it, and tried to bring some of the light of the gospel into their lives. Some youth minsters have seen their role as understanding youth culture and behaving in a way which tries to convince young people that they are still living their lives in that culture – which they really left behind years ago. If you are 30, why try to convince young people you are still 21? Once anybody stops living and breathing in a cultural setting, they do not really feel or understand it. There are leaders who think they do, and they are not doing young people any favours as role models. Our task is to do as Paul did – try our best to understand their world and challenge it where it needs to be challenged (not everything), so that they see how to live in their world with gospel values. In other words, there are times when we need to be countercultural. David Jackman, former leader of the Cornhill Training Course, once said that we should preach with the Bible in one hand and a newspaper in the other. David would not give those two documents equal weight, but his statement is a reminder that we should teach with an awareness of what is happening in our world if we are to help young people know what is right and wrong. Maybe all youth ministers should watch the news or read a paper and maybe even watch *EastEnders* or *Hollyoaks*.

There are some programmes on the TV which are supposed to be a reflection of youth culture, but they are only there to shock and thereby increase audience figures. They are not a picture of how the majority of young people behave. It is rare that dramas deal honestly with social issues – they are screened at a time when the inter-channel ratings war is at its height. But let us never minimize the influence of soaps on our young people. They watch them and talk about them the next morning. (The Damaris Trust has some excellent material which helps young people and leaders reflect on the values underpinning the soaps, and how to respond to what they portray – see www.damaris.org.)

## Gospel v. Culture

It is not my purpose to do a thorough evaluation of youth culture, but within our core purpose of teaching the Bible we need to be aware of how it might influence young people's response to God's Word. An obvious example is their attitude to pre-marital sexual activity. The soaps give the idea that sex is what you do if you are in love, or if you feel like it. The Bible says sex is for marriage and we should wait until that marriage ceremony has been held 'before witnesses and in the presence of God'. Here are some more issues which create a tension with a biblical world-view

| CULTURE | GOSPEL |
|---|---|
| Variable Morality | Fixed morality |
| Internal authority | External authority |
| Non-book culture | Based on a book |
| Easygoing – 'cool' | Hard work |
| Peer group | Individual salvation |
| . . . | . . . |

Maybe you'd like to add a few more values where culture and the gospel clash.

Generally our culture is suggesting that morality is a matter of choice, whereas the gospel insists that, because God loves us, he has created boundaries for our good. Much modern psychology suggests that children and young people thrive if boundaries are clear – our task is to help young people make the transition from the rightly enforced boundaries of childhood to the autonomy of adult life where choices will have to be made on their own. If we have made that transition in a biblical framework then the child will be keen to know what God's will is for their lives and what it means to live and think 'Christianly'. Youth culture gives each young person room to decide their own moral stance (variable morality), but the gospel makes moral behaviour a clear statement about obedience to God's commands (fixed morality). As adulthood approaches, young people will be called upon to make more and more choices about their lives and encouraged to think that they are the only authority. Each person has internalized authority and ceases to take their lead from any external authority, whereas the gospel is based on a book which tells God's story and lovingly lays out for us how we should live. But the life of a young person is much less book-orientated. God's book, the Bible, carries the full weight of the God who made heaven and earth – we are his children so we do what our Father says. Whether we live in a book culture or not, the Bible retains its authority on all matters of faith and conduct.

**THINK AND ACT**

- What are the main influences (positive and negative) on the young people in your youth group?
- What are the key areas where culture and gospel values clash for young people today?

## What is youth culture?

It is much more than the sum of music, DVDs, soaps, computer games, chat rooms, magazines and movies which young people indulge in. Some have defined it as the air that young people breathe; it is all around them and they take it in just as unconsciously as oxygen. Each group they enter, each game they play, each conversation has the potential to influence their world-view and morality. It should be a priority for youth ministers to at least make themselves aware of the content of the material that young people read, listen to or watch. We should also realize that culture never remains static. It is influenced by fashion, and that is market-driven and always on the move. I served as a youth minister in western Sheffield, and before that as a teacher in a school in north-west Sheffield. The two areas were no more than four miles apart, but the young people were very different. In one area, if Sheffield Wednesday lost one was wise to remain silent, whilst the youth from the other area cared very little about any football teams, but were more inclined towards Sheffield United. Their post-school expectations were different, as were their music tastes. It must also be noted that such things as musical taste move on very fast, mainly in response to airplay time. Youth culture is always in transition, and many young people struggle to keep up with the trends which have largely been set in the marketplace.

So, in broad terms, what is the impact of youth culture?

### 1. Youth culture influences behaviour

The most obvious area is in the area of sexual behaviour. It assumes that sexual activity for teenagers is the way to be cool: 'Everybody's doing it, so why shouldn't I?' Magazines talk more of being careful than they talk about abstinence. Advice can be given to teenagers about how to please your partner whether gay or straight, and information can be presented without any standard of absolute morality. It is all about how you feel or whether your partner is in the mood or has stopped fancying you.

### 2. Youth culture creates image

To a teenager image is everything, and to express who you are by your appearance matters a great deal. For some that will be the latest designer clothes, for others it will be the gothic look, whilst others will go for body piercing. Magazines are full of beautiful people and, although most images have been computer-enhanced, their readers still long to look like the glossy pictures. Your significance and your value to the community are measured by what you own or what you achieve through academic success, sporting talent, or creative ability. In some extreme cases, criminal activity is a path to social acceptance. What you look like matters; if you are not one of the beautiful people, you are not worth much. As Christians, we believe each person is made uniquely by God in his image; we are his workmanship and are valued. Surely this is something we must teach to young people whose self-esteem has been battered by the marketing gurus.

### 3. Youth culture exploits through the media

Both of the previous pressure points have their impact through the media. Natural development by the teenager is made to look abnormal – you can become beautiful much more quickly if you use this cosmetic or that treatment. The teenage market is a huge money-spinner. Ellen Widdup (quoting a study conducted by the Office of National Statistics) writing in the *Evening Standard* in March 2009 said that the lifestyle of British teens cost £9,000 per annum; most of the young people own laptops, TVs, DVD players and iPods, spend over £1,000 a year on mobiles, MP3s and downloads, £300 on trainers and £240 on haircuts, as well as spending money on expensive clothing and nights out.

The young person cannot possibly miss out on wearing that gear or smelling gorgeous. Adverts are put on at the right teenage viewing times (the market knows exactly when to screen them) and word passes around the in-crowd that this product will transform their lives; they cannot afford to miss out. The need for acceptance is manipulated into a product-based desire rather than a desire for wholesome relationships. There are teenagers who really believe they will never be happy unless they wear a certain T-shirt or smell like a perfume shop every minute of every day.

**4. Youth culture entertains**

If you watch a teenage hero on the TV you will be entertained. TV is not 'cool' if it informs (that's for school), but it is 'very cool' to have a laugh and be happy. Sad people are not 'cool' so entertainment must be light. When the character Jim Robinson died in the Australian soap *Neighbours*, his heart attack was only mentioned in the next few episodes and then he was forgotten because death was not 'happy'. We all like to watch entertaining television, and that's fine, but there are other things on the TV which will be watched by young people in their own rooms. Every house in the UK has, on average, 2.4 TVs operating per home. That has to mean that many children have a TV in their own room and can watch movies the censor has said they cannot watch.

**5. Youth culture says you need to belong**

Every teenager has a strong urge to belong to something. To have friends is vital and to keep in contact with them is crucial. The guy who invented the mobile phone with the text message facility knew the generation that would drive its development. Most young people are given strong messages that they must be individuals, but not so way out that they do not fit with the rest of their tribe. They constantly live in the tension (created by the media) that they must be their own person and merge in well with their peers.

Some aspects of popular culture can have a positive influence upon our young people. Some of the clothes they buy certainly look better than those I had as a teenager, even though some cannot afford them. Not all music is bad – I still enjoy some bands, but the lyrics of some songs portray, at best, a sub-Christian world-view. The key word is discernment. I can see no problem with young people buying and using cosmetic products, but the marketing of these products is geared to creating dependency on them. It is possible for them to buy the media version of true happiness.

These are just some statements which sum up the values of popular youth culture

- If I am beautiful I am worthwhile.
- I want nothing to do with pain – if it gets to me, I want immediate medical treatment.
- Sex exists as part of recreation; to be active is normal and there will be no consequences.
- It is all right to sort out disagreements with violence.
- It is acceptable to manipulate family and friends in order to get what I want.
- Money is the only route to true happiness.
- Society has no future, so live for today – I may as well.
- Meeting my personal needs is what I deserve, and that is more important than anything else in my life.

## Peer pressure

There comes a time where parents are regarded by their offspring as first-class village idiots because they know little or nothing about the world their children inhabit. One of the key things parents find so hard to deal with is when their children say, 'My friends understand me better than my parents do.' Young people will say they can be who they really are in the company of friends, but feel awkward with their parents. This is all part of natural development. Children start out in life by being completely dependent on their parents, but as soon as they attend something such as a play group they get to know other children and become friends. At first, parents are very much in the picture when these friends come to the house. But it's not long before children go to a birthday party without their parents, and then spend five days a week at school, and go away on their first residential. By the time secondary school arrives, they want to hang out with mates, and parents find out that they have been seen with a member of the opposite sex.

From play group to youth group, our children come under the influence of other children. Some of those children will have more influence than others. The best footballer in the year group will be listened to, as will the most attractive girl in Year 8.

This growing move from parent dependency to peer group influence has its dangers, as the chosen group may or may not be a positive influence. The need for acceptance will drive the need to fit in with the values of that group. If our youth group fails to provide that peer group, then the young people will look elsewhere for acceptance. I believe we should start to provide that group from the age of 7 at the latest. The 7 to 10 group which meets to get to know each other, have fun and listen to the stories of the Bible is vital if young people are to remain connected to the local church. Once secondary school starts, peer groups are often well established and their influence has started to bite. Our church recently ran a week away for the 15+ group during GCSE results week. One member of the group wanted to go home not to find out her own results (which were stunning), but to find out her friends'. What happened to her friends really mattered to her. If young people were left to choose their secondary school, where their friends went would be the decisive factor.

There are other influences on the lives of young people. What is the role of parents, and how can the church be a place which helps the growth of young disciples? There are no simple answers to these issues, but we must pray that God would enable us to help young people through the moral maze they face – perhaps if we were more upfront about our own struggles it would help our young people grow in Christ. We are not helped by preachers who make it sound as if they have their feet on such solid ground they don't even know the word 'temptation'. Our own vulnerability will help young people realize there is a battle out there to remain God's faithful soldiers and servants, and some cultural values will undermine us if we are not careful. We must tell them what God's Word says, to give them a map and compass to chart their course: 'We . . . share . . . the gospel [and] our lives as well, because you had become so dear to us' (1 Thess. 2:8, NIV).

## THINK AND ACT

Think about your young people.

- What are they watching?
- What are they reading?
- What are they buying?
- Who are their friends? (Mainly Christian or not?)
- Do they have a mobile phone?
- Are they into social networking?
- What aspects of popular culture could you use positively in the youth group? For example, how could you use texting or Facebook?
- What negative aspects of popular culture are the young people in your youth group dealing with?
- How can you help young people think 'Christianly' about these issues?

# CREATING AN ENVIRONMENT

4.

# Growing Up: A Place to Become Christians

We now return to those four keys aspects of youth ministry we defined in the first chapter – becoming, growing, living and serving as Christians. The next three chapters explore key activities which should be part of any biblically based youth group. At the heart of all of these we will find ways in which God's Word stimulates our youth to be obedient people. If we have found out God's purposes from his Word, then we must act on them if he really is our Lord.

## Growth is normal

The usual starting point for evangelism is Jesus' words in the great commission

> Therefore go and make disciples of all nations, baptizing them in the name of the Father and of the Son and of the Holy Spirit, teaching them to observe all that I have commanded you. And behold, I am with you always, to the end of the age.
>
> (Matt. 28:19,20)

or the description of the early church: 'And the Lord added to their number day by day those who were being saved' (Acts 2:47).

This has to be one of the most disobeyed commands of Jesus – we simply don't do this, and to raise the topic of evangelism in some churches is a real turn-off. Despite the promise of Jesus that he would always be with us, and we say that Jesus is the best thing that has ever happened to us, we are reluctant to talk about him. The Bible gives us clear definitions; that means that a large percentage (over 90 per cent) of the population of the UK are lost, and the Bible says that is serious. So if we have listened to God's Word we have no alternative but to help people become disciples. How do we help our young people be God's ambassadors (see Eph. 6:20)? Is it too much to expect our young people to speak and act in ways which will display the fact that they belong to Christ? Many of them hang out in hostile environments and their main aim is to merge into the background, not stand out in a crowd.

Perhaps the 'all nations' phrase of Matthew 28 has convinced us that evangelism happens abroad, so young people can go to Africa for a gap year. Evangelism at home doesn't have quite the same ring to it. It's very easy to convince ourselves that this job is for the fanatic or the one who is the ultra keen member of the youth group. But Peter does not allow us to wriggle out of our calling so easily

> Always being prepared to make a defence to anyone who asks you for a reason for the hope that is in you; yet do it with gentleness and respect
>
> (1 Pet. 3:15)

It is clear from the context of this verse that Peter is not talking about the gift of being an evangelist. Not everybody has that gift. In the first part of the verse he says 'in your hearts honour Christ the Lord as holy' – we all should do that and, if we do, what we say and how we act will honour the name of Jesus. I have a close friend who is a retired bank manager. He would never claim to be the world's leading apologist, but when I went to get my tyres changed the man asked me what I did for a living. I told him I was a minister in a church just up the road. His immediate response was to ask if this was the church where my bank manager friend attended. He told me how straight and honest he was in all his dealings – 'That's a man with a real faith,' said the tyre man. The integrity of his business dealings had spoken volumes about his faith. He is in his seventies, but still effective. We have a 16-year-old in her youth group who asked to be baptized. She had invited her friends from school. In the youth meeting after the service, one of her friends became a Christian. We have just heard about a child who brought six friends to a club for primary school children.

It is all about the attitude of the heart, and the realization that 'lost people matter to God' as Bill Hybels of Willow Creek Community Church in Chicago is often heard saying.

## Who does the work of an evangelist?

The answer is very simple – *all of us*. And whether we do it by proclamation or presence, we all have an effect on the people we rub shoulders with every day. We can't help it; we are what we are so people around us make judgements about us, our behaviour and our values.

We must never become critical of how effective our young people are in sharing their faith – the example they get from adults is not always effective. But what hinders young people (and adults) from doing that work?

- Being unaware we have to.
  It is a command to be obeyed and one that cannot be avoided – do we really think that God created his church (and youth groups) for maintenance only? Are we so busy meeting up with Christian friends that we have completely lost contact with any unbelievers? Evangelism is not always comfortable, but it is clearly biblical.
- Not sure about what we believe.
  Our lack of understanding means we feel we would fail in any encounter with a not-yet Christian. We are not sure about the basic doctrines of the faith; maybe we would benefit from a course in Christian basics.

- Not caring about people.
  Jonathan Lamb once said[1] that if we were truly convinced about the reality of a lost eternity, we would never stop speaking about Jesus. Jesus came to 'seek and save [the] lost' (Luke 19:10, NIV), and we should not allow our hearts to grow cold. Is it possible for us to get so involved with 'churchianity' that we stop doing Christianity. Young people can become so absorbed in the life of the group that they try to forget the 'lost world' that surrounds them.
- Finding it hard to speak.
  Not all of us are natural chatterers; we all have friends and family that we know and care about, but we lack the confidence to speak. Perhaps we miss the last bit of Matthew 28 because Jesus promised he would be with us until the end of the world. We never speak of Christ alone; his Spirit is always with us and he will give us words that we might find surprising if we see this only as a human activity. It is God who speaks through his servants who are empowered by the Holy Spirit. A failure to see that dynamic will make us worry about failure rather than wanting to be faithful and obedient.
- Fear of mockery.
  This is a genuine fear – none of us like to lose friends but if we love our friends, as I hope we do, then shouldn't we offer them the best deal we know? Even if that leads to temporary or permanent separation, we have been faithful to God. (That does not mean we present the gospel in an abrasive way so as to deliberately lose friends.)
- No opportunities
  This is a difficult one to face, but have we become so immersed in church things that we try to minimize any contact with the secular world. They regard us as

slightly strange and we regard them as a potential stain on our otherwise holy existence. Acts 2:47 (and other places) tells us the early church had 'favour with all the people'. They were highly regarded – the next phrase says 'the Lord added to their number day by day those who were being saved.'

We must talk about these barriers with our young people and train them to be more effective. Very few people are natural chatterers and we all need help – young and old.

Luke, the writer of Acts, is trying to tell us that people in a good relationship with their community have an evangelistic impact. But for our young people, their environment of school can be hostile. It can be a place they don't enjoy and, if we tell our students to be bold in their witness, they say they just want to fit in. All they want is to keep their friends sweet and not give them any reason to dump them. The last thing they want to do is stand out. I'm not sure adults are any better at this sort of thing in their own workplace.

**THINK AND ACT**

Think about

- What stops you/your group from being effective in evangelism?
- What are you/your group's greatest fears about witnessing?

So how can we make our youth group a place where we should expect people to become Christians? I was heavily involved in the Billy Graham missions in the UK in the

1980s. Those events saw many young people become Christians. I believe young people are as open to the gospel now as they were then. Maybe that method is not for today, but we have recently seen significant numbers of young people respond to a 'mass' event in our own city of Winchester. My one concern with these is that it stops us thinking evangelistically for the rest of the year. University students can get very motivated about their biannual mission, but soon hide after a frenetic week of food, 'grill a Christian', and questionnaires. It has ceased to be part of every week's programme. I am not suggesting we have gospel appeals at every meeting of our youth group, but I am suggesting that evangelism is not an activity, it is a *value* – it's part of the way we breathe. We should not be surprised that new people appear in our group to see what this Christian thing is all about. One answer to this has been the big gathering where we have a worship band, some video input, a really punchy talk at the end, and then invite response. These do have merit, but do young people who respond become disappointed when they join up with their much smaller and less trendy youth group?

Here are some pointers to an effective strategy we can use to train young people to be effective in evangelism.

## Teach

You should not be surprised at this. If we are to send our young people into a world that knows little or nothing about God, we must send them out equipped. If they are to engage with the people in their world, the first thing they need to know is what the good news is and how it is the command of God to share it. Not everyone in your group will be able to master the full theological complexities of the atonement, but most of them know they don't always do the things they wish they did (Rom. 7:15–25). Most of them, with some helpful teaching, will be able to give a basic version of the gospel story. We might say, 'God is a beautiful person – you can be beautiful too!' but that is not the gospel. (If you think I made up that awful phrase, I didn't – I actually heard it with my own ears!)

We need to give our youth the foundational truths of the gospel.

- God is the God of creation who made human beings just like us to live on the beautiful earth he created.
- Because he is God (and we will never be that) he tells us to obey his commands and live in the ways he made us to live.
- Men and women choose to disobey God by ignoring his commands and denying his word – 'Did God really say' (Gen. 3:1, NIV).
- Humanity now has a problem – God is holy and cannot be approached by sinful people, which we all are and have been from the start of our lives.
- We cannot solve the problem of restoring relationship with God.
- God takes the initiative in sending his only Son, who as 'God in a body' lives on the planet with the people who have disobeyed.
- God allows his one and only perfect Son to take upon himself the sin of the world so whoever believes that he did it for them becomes one whom God forgives – the relationship is restored.
- It's still only partial, but Jesus rises from the dead to show us the way out of this sinful world.
- Christ's return to his Father is the guarantee that one day, when we die or when he comes back, we will be with him for ever.

I'm sure many of you have better and slicker ways of explaining the gospel, but the heart of it needs to be communicated over and over again. Young people need to ask questions if they don't understand something. Booklets such as *Two Ways to Live*[2] can help. It's good to take some time to share with each other, and role plays can help as long they don't become stereotyped.

## Train

There's more to this than giving them a two-minute soundbite to spout as soon as an unbeliever comes into view. Most good faith-sharing experiences are conversations. We must learn to be good listeners and train our young people to be the same. As they talk to someone, suggest they listen to what their friend is saying. As they engage in conversation, encourage them to pick up on the barrier that is keeping them from following Christ. There are training courses in evangelism techniques, but they should be treated as helpful guidelines rather than a ready-made script. We need to help our youth to be sensitive to the person they are talking to – their friend may have just lost a loved one, or suffered the divorce or separation of their parents. That is their big issue. We cannot ignore such events and should try to build from their story, but always be conscious that God's story of salvation is the one they need to hear whatever experiences dominate their lives.

I Thessalonians 2:8 reminds us that we are to share 'the gospel . . . but our lives as well' (NIV) and, in any conversation, we should try to strike that balance. A simple gospel summary is good to have stored away. It may not be appropriate in our first conversation, but should surface very soon. It is easy to drift into long-term sympathy to make a friend feel good. We may then delay any talk of the gospel for as long as we can. In the end, that is not the purpose of the conversation, although we should always be seeking to build relationships with our friends. If we love someone, we want the best for them, and the best for them is knowing Jesus. We are God's voice on this earth – his voice must not remain silent as we are faithful to the command to be his witnesses.

## Model

There is a spiritual gift of being an evangelist. As it is a gift, not all of us will have it. But we are all called to be witnesses, and we all have networks of friends and acquaintances. You can find out about yours by making a copy of this diagram and putting some names into each box. Put your name in the central box

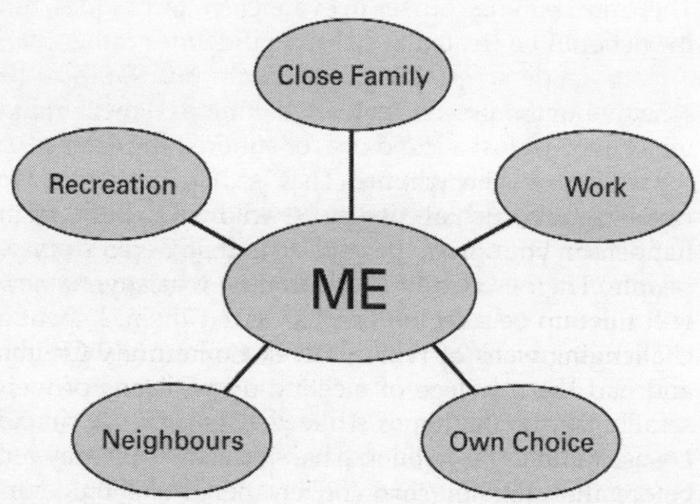

If my youth are to get excited about faith-sharing, then they have to see me *doing* it. At this point, my guilt is considerable as I can get so involved with the Christian world of committees and maintenance that it is easy to lose any contact with the secular world. I have a golfing friend who is well into his seventies and still plays a mean game. He is a late convert to the Christian faith (through an Alpha course). He is a retired senior army officer and, at his ruby wedding, invited around thirty people – ten ex-army friends, ten golfing chums and ten friends from the church. He may be well advanced in years, but he has seen the way we must model the faith to others and I must do the same if young people are to see that it works. In Sheffield, our young people gathered friends at several houses, ate a lot of pizza, showed a video, and then talked about it. The leaders' team met in my cellar to pray. Several young people joined the group from that evening.

## Structure

How is our ministry set up? If a new person turns up, what happens? Do they stand there looking lost, with the well-established cliques closed to newcomers, all the regulars making small talk and cracking in-jokes? If that happens in your group it is not structured to receive new people. There is also little expectation that anyone new will turn up because no one has asked them. I spent a challenging week at Willow Creek Community Church and had the privilege of meeting up with one of their small groups a few times. They were a great bunch and I was invited to Starbucks, had breakfast and prayed before they left for school. They prayed at the gates before they went in to school that God would give them the opportunity to have significant conversations with their friends and that they would be able to invite them to their youth group at the weekend. Whenever they met as a small group there was an empty chair which signified that the group was never complete. You can dismiss that as rather corny, but I have never been in a group of young people who had such a passion to see their friends become Christians.

That is what I mean by 'structure'. It's not too hard for any Christian to invite a friend. There must be something in your programme where the guest can feel at home and people talk to them. Is your meeting's content such that it alienates the new arrival? It's one reason why I believe there should be some social interaction built into any programme. In my discipleship groups, we often had a night out which would be at a bowling alley or a 'scoff as much as you like pizza house' where it was easy to invite a friend.

One day at Christ Church Fulwood we realized, after many months, that scores of young people walked past the church on their way home to eat dinner, watch *Neighbours* and do their homework. One of our leaders created a weekly diversion by way of a coffee and tea bar with large supplies of excellent cakes made by church members. There was no obvious spiritual content such as a talk; simply unconditional friendship and good food. We left Christian material around on tables and it often got taken. After a few weeks there were significant conversations, and some of our guests came to join us at our weekend group meetings. We had structured an easy way in for our young people to bring friends, which had a low cringe factor.

If we put on a massive all-singing all-dancing event, far removed from what we'd normally do, then we should not be surprised that, having been dragged along to the big gig, young people are not too keen on our very different group meetings. If friendship and openness is offered, together with a willingness to engage with them as people, we have a realistic structure.

## Value

Our young people look to us as leaders to see what we value, so our attitude to evangelism is key. I have been in groups where those who get all the attention and plaudits are the loud, attractive or able people. In a crowd of youth, it is easy to miss those who want to live a godly life and are working with their friends, trying to help them to follow Jesus. If they see that evangelism matters to you, it will become a value of your group, not an occasional bolt-on activity. '. . . the Lord added to their number day by day those who were being saved' (Acts 2:47) is not the experience of most churches, because we have lost the vision that the church (and the youth group) should be expanding.

I once took a young man on one of my preaching engagements. It was a country church with a long history of gospel ministry, but was now dying with an ageing congregation. My friend had never spoken in public before but he had come, as a first attempt, to read the Bible in the service. We were greeted by the elders, and I was asked what the passage was for this evening – I told them, and that my friend was going to read the lesson. I was emphatically informed that all readings in the church must be from the Authorised Version – no other version could be read. My friend had spent hours reading his lesson over and over in the NIV translation. He would have been completely thrown if he had tried to read it from the rather large pulpit Bible. For the sake of that young man's development, would it have been worth a compromise? These elders were having none of it. I ended up reading my own lesson and the drive home was rather sad. He had not been valued and was 'off church' for quite a few weeks after that.

We must value our young people, and support and encourage in them the things that really matter. So we have to notice when someone brings a friend, and tell them they've done a good job. In the group we talk about the fact that it's great when we meet new friends. We do not allow young people to 'clique' their way through youth group and give big sloppy hugs to all and sundry and the new arrival feels out of it. You can't stop girls and boys being attracted to each other (that's natural) but if an 'item' (that's a boy/girl relationship) becomes a dominant feature in the group, it needs to be toned down.

In my younger married years, I had a voracious appetite which I now have to watch to avoid becoming a walking barrel. I was described as 'an ever-open door' – that is a good label for a group committed to being a place where people become Christians.

# 5.

# A Place to Learn How to Live and Grow as Christians

There is a process called *growing up*. Some of us wish it never happened. Others of us act as if it never has! But however we like or dislike the process, we do pass from babyhood to childhood to adolescence and on into adulthood whether we act like it or not. The Bible never speaks of a person standing still in their Christian growth – Paul had this longing that people would become *mature*: 'Brothers, do not be children in your thinking. Be infants in evil, but in your thinking be mature' (1 Cor. 14:20), '. . . until we attain to the unity of the faith and of the knowledge of the Son of God, to mature manhood' (Eph. 4:13).

And another of Paul's comments is about his aim in ministry: 'Him (Jesus) we proclaim, warning everyone and teaching everyone with all wisdom, that we may present everyone mature in Christ' (Col. 1:28).

How many 'everyones' in this verse do we need to be convinced that maturity is the goal of ministry and not the preservation of childish things? Our longing must be to see our young people grow into men and women of God who will be his 'faithful soldiers and servants to the end of their days' (Anglican Book of Common Worship – Order for Baptism). One of the great joys in leading the Keswick Convention youth ministry has been seeing young people come to the age of 18 and join us as leaders in the programme. In my own church in Winchester, we could not run children's ministry without the contribution of our youth group members. That needs to be seen as normal. What kind of growth are we looking for? Numerical growth, as we have seen, is part of what we do, but as soon as we have new believers our longing should be the same as Peter's that people will '. . . grow in the grace and knowledge of our Lord and Saviour Jesus Christ' (2 Pet. 3:18).

Peter wants believers both to grow in their character and in the knowledge (and wisdom) that comes from knowing Jesus Christ. There are many examples of these kinds of verses in the New Testament (Why not try to find some more?). So we must assume this was a major activity in the early church as Christian communities sprang up around the Mediterranean. New believers must not stand still. Members of the early church would have been, by definition, new believers, so helping people mature would have been a top priority – perhaps we have become so 'established' that we have forgotten that new believers still need help in growing up. And not just new believers – young people who have grown up in the care of Christian parents still have to grow in maturity

**THINK AND ACT**

- How much of your group activity is geared to the intentional making of disciples?
- Take a look at the members of your group – are they growing as Christians?

So how is growth into maturity to be achieved? Some believe that all you need to do is just hang around Christian groups and you'll sort of catch on to what Jesus wants from you. It is said that all the people in the group are so like Jesus (and their leaders) in their behaviour that you really can't miss him. I'm so glad that the young people who have been part of groups I have led have *not* had to rely on me being such a good image of Jesus that they just learned how to live just by watching me. I am very capable of teaching error (not deliberately), and I can be short with people, ignore them, be sarcastic and wish that I was anywhere but in the group meeting. If young people had to rely on me for their picture of Jesus they would get a rough deal sometimes! That it is not to say I should not strive to reflect the words and actions of Jesus in everything I do. On balance, I hope I have been more of a positive role model than a negative one, but I've had my bad days

Every disciple of Jesus has to learn how to grow – to develop their understanding of the Scriptures, to learn how to pray and to deal with the flaws in their character which every person has. Have you sat in talks where you have been asked if your love for God has grown cold? I have, and have been astonished how many speakers give you no idea how to rekindle the fire. So you go home convinced your love for God has completely vanished and you will find it very hard to get it back. I believe we shall see young Christians grow if we give them a stimulating programme of teaching which connects with them and their world and helps them to live in it. In our talks and Bible studies we must apply the passages of Scripture to their lives to convince them that the Bible has everything to say about their existence. We must tell them what Jesus said about issues of sex and marriage, handling wealth, who is my neighbour, how we worship and so on. You will never run out of things to teach and don't be afraid to tackle the social injustice of Amos or the battles in the Old Testament where God instructed his people to wipe out cities. Remember 'All Scripture is . . . profitable' (2 Tim. 3:16), and if we avoid parts of the Bible, our young people will assume it's OK for them to ignore bits they don't like.

## Being intentional

Much of the youth ministry I have witnessed is based on a kind of worldly hope. We hope our young people will come back to church, and attendance has become the main objective. As long as they're sitting there we're happy – we have a tick in our register. We drift into maintenance mode so readily that we stop asking the crucial question. What elements in our programme are designed to help young people mature in Christ? To put it another way – what are the issues that are stifling their growth, and how are we dealing with those issues? Have we ever sat down in a one-to-one with members of our youth group and asked them how they're doing and, when we hear they are not flourishing, done something about it? It is easy to see service as evidence of growth – it may be, but it may also be covering up real issues. If they're helping in the crèche or the Sunday school they must be doing fine. Activity may not be the same as maturity.

David Watson wrote

> If we were willing to learn the real way of discipleship and actually become disciples, the church in the west would be transformed and the resultant impact on society would be staggering.[1]

It is essential to 'preach the word' so that young people learn what God is saying, but it is also crucial to have leaders around who can talk and listen in small groups or in one-to-ones. Youth groups need to have teaching programmes which give young people an understanding of the scriptural truth. But so often this gives rise to questions, so your group needs people who can give young people time to answer and discuss them. It is preferable that their regular leaders can give them time – the leader gets to know a genuine enquiry from a red herring and, once the relationship is established, is able to ask the hard mentoring questions as well as give encouragement, prayer and support. Young people appreciate genuine human beings who will be honest and clear with them. My own children, when I was the leader of the youth ministry in our church, all had significant adults who fulfilled the role which I could not. I was their father and needed to remain as that. Such relationships are crucial in the life of young people, and if we simply bombard them with teaching and give no room for dialogue, then we are in danger of stifling their growth.

I am sure that an hour every two weeks (or whatever you are able to give) would be a huge investment of time in young people's lives. It would hopefully be fruitful for the young person, but also give the leader insights about the real issues facing the youth who listen to their teaching. Your hour could look something like this

- Choose a place where you are unlikely to be disturbed.
- Only meet with someone of the same gender.
- Open with a short prayer. Ask for the guidance of the Holy Spirit, and for a useful time together.
- Briefly share experiences over the last week – reflect on what was talked about in your last meeting, and whether those issues had been a struggle or went well.
- Open up a passage of Scripture. I would suggest you don't jump about everywhere, but take a book and read right through it in your meetings for a few weeks. Look for biblical principles as well as specific commands to be obeyed. Enjoy looking at how great our God is.
- Try to leave your friend with an assignment for the following week based on the passage you have studied. Ask the question, 'What does this passage suggest I need to put into action right now?'
- Pray together – thank God for what you have learned, ask him for strength to live for him in the coming week.
- Pray for each other in the time between your meetings.

A disciple is one who is personally called by Jesus: 'Follow *me*, and I will make you become fishers of men' (Mark 1:17, my italics). This would suggest that Jesus spent one-to-one (or small-group time) with his disciples. He sat down and taught them even when the crowds were hanging on his every word. He knew they would be faced with pressures and temptations, and he wanted them to be ready. He knew it would not be easy for them so he told them countercultural and helpful things: 'You have heard that it was said . . . But I say to you' (Matt. 5:43–44). In other words, the culture, although it may not be inherently evil, is not our primary source for learning about how to live. *Jesus* is and he is the living Word, encapsulated for us in the written Word.

## 24/7 disciples

Learning to follow Jesus Christ day by day is not the same as

- Being a church member
- Sitting in a pew on Sunday
- Singing in the worship band
- Reading your Bible every day out of duty

  etc.

All these things are fine in themselves but they are about what we *do*, not about who we *are*. I am convinced that one of the major factors in the exodus of young people from our churches is that we have failed to help them grow in their faith. We have made the assumption that if we take them to enough Christian gigs or festivals they will keep going. If we give them a job to do, that will keep them coming. I believe this misses the point. Christian maturity has always been taught and learned by the disciple (the word means 'follower'). We must be completely intentional about that process and deal with doubts and questions honestly and openly. We long to see the response that Jesus got from the men of Galilee: 'At once they left their nets and followed him' (Mark 1:18, NIV).

**THINK AND ACT**

- Make a list of the things that lead members of your youth group away from following Jesus.
- What stops young people giving their total allegiance to Jesus?
- Do we make too many demands on our young people – are we making it too hard for them to follow Christ?

For many young people, being a disciple is not easy. What TV programmes are not good for a Christian to watch? Does *Friends* portray a world-view which is unhelpful? What sort of parties are 'off-limits' for Christians? None of these questions will have a direct answer in the Bible – nowhere does the Word of God say, 'Thou shalt not watch *Friends*.' What can and can't be done has to be worked out by each person who faces those issues, but their decisions need to be based on a biblical world-view. So often young people want to know boundaries in these issues – boundaries can be helpful, but there may be a better way. If we are truly in a relationship with Jesus Christ and we know that he loves us, what better motive can there be than to do all we can to please him? Rather than asking, 'How far can I go without getting God angry at me?' we should train our young people to say, 'What is it about this relationship that would please Jesus above all else?' Let's look at a couple of scenarios.

***16-year-old girl in a relationship with a 17-year-old boy***

- Both attend the youth group.
- They go out together.
- Their love for each other seems genuine.

**What questions should they be asking?**

- What sexual boundaries need to be set so we honour God with our bodies?
- Do we make time for other members of the group, or are we too wrapped up in each other?
- What time do we spend talking about God and praying together?
- Do we bring out the best in each other that encourages both of us to follow Christ?

**15-year-old boy attending the youth group – parents not Christians**

- Parents are not antagonistic – they hope he will get over it soon.
- They come to church at Christmas.
- They hope their son will make a good lawyer (his present career choice).

**What questions should he be asking?**

- How often do I pray for my parents?
- Do I go to youth group too often, and should I honour my parents by spending more time at home?
- Do I need friends at church to pray for me?
- Should I tidy my room more often?

Neither of those lists of questions is complete – there are many more questions they should be asking. But, if they are following Christ, those are the areas which need exploration.

## Creating a world-view

Are we just telling our young people how they should behave and what they should watch? Are we creating a series of rules and regulations – that if you follow them, you'll be safe and secure in Christ? That sounds like a 'tick box approach' which gives the person the choice, depending on what they feel at that moment. We do *not* want them to ask the question, 'What can I get away with before God gets cross with me?'

Most of them, by the time they get to 18, will be free to watch whatever their remote control can access. They will be free to go out where they choose and behave as they wish. Here is one of the great dilemmas of our teaching and learning. Young people need to develop discernment about what is 'of good report' (Phil. 4:8, NKJV) and be able to tell the difference themselves. If it is blasphemous, you need a good reason to keep watching or reading that material. If it offends God it should offend any believer, and we are trying to get our young people to know for themselves what is good and right. If laughter is created out of mocking another person then it cannot be right. It contradicts the precept that everyone is precious in the eyes of God and should be cherished. I remember laughing till I cried watching one of Peter Kay's stage shows; he had picked up on the idiosyncrasies of people he had observed, but I don't think he degraded them. If we have persuaded young people that you can look at something and, because they have developed standards of their own, decide to turn it off or watch it, we have helped them to think

Christianly. I once got in real trouble with a bunch of parents when I told them they should watch *EastEnders* with their kids and then talk about the issues the programme raised. They need help to know if *EastEnders* should be turned off.

**QUICK THINK**

- Should you ever encourage young people to turn off a TV programme? On what basis?

Computers need some kind of supervision. Whether it is wicked men seeking inappropriate relationships or an obsession with pornography, we need to warn them about the first and be clear about the second. Young people must be told that there are people who will exploit them given half a chance. I am writing this a few days after a woman in Plymouth who ran a children's nursery has been convicted of abusing children – the Bible is clear that we must *warn* our young people against such exploitation. Unhelpful websites are so easy to access that we have a duty to tell our youth that they can guard against such evil material seeping into their lives.

### The big issue

If you've failed to spot that the young person's world is full of sexual imagery, which planet have you been living on? As teenagers, they are living through the period of their lives where sexual awareness is running at full speed. The soppy girls of childhood have become very attractive and the boys have noticed it. The sweet little blond boy is fancied by half the girls in the youth group. To talk of sex as being for marriage is hard to swallow when many will hear boasting about sexual experience, and how many girls they pulled during the weekend. And please don't think that doesn't happen in Christian groups. In Josh McDowell's work on teenage sexuality in the 1980s, an often quoted statistic was that 25 per cent of Christian young people had had sex by the age of 18. Young people desperately need help in this area. We need to set the standard but we must give the reason. 'Thou shalt not commit adultery' is not the statement of a cosmic killjoy – it is the statement of a loving Father who created sex within his boundaries of stable relationships. We must explain to our young people that we don't have sex to get a rating so we can compare how good we are with others. Sex is God's gift to express our love to a person within the confines of marriage. It is meant to be enjoyed because God made it that way. One of the purposes of sex was to procreate. Children need stable relationships – that's why God said that sex was for marriage where there would, ideally, be a secure relationship. *Please* explain this to your group so that they don't think it's good to try a few people out in bed before finally commiting to one who's good at it. It could just be the reason why we have a growing rate of divorce and teenage pregnancy when people find that the experiment is over, but the poor girl is lumbered with a baby she really didn't want. Or the magic has faded, and the new girl at school looks far more attractive than the one you finally managed to get into bed. We need to hear and understand the sexual language and behaviour of the teenager and teach positively. Not just God's standards, but also the purpose behind them. Love is God's idea, and he knows where it works and doesn't work.

We need to be clear and positive about the biblical standards given to us by a loving God for our good because we want our young people to grow as Christians by living as Christians.

> Finally, brothers, whatever is true, whatever is honourable, whatever is just, whatever is pure, whatever is lovely, whatever is commendable, if there is any excellence, if there is anything worthy of praise, think about these things.
>
> (Phil. 4:8)

We cannot allow young people to wallow around in their world and hope they make all the right decisions about what is true and noble. They need some clarity from us and help in knowing what is going to build them up as believers. They also need to know they can come to us as their leader and talk about their experiences. We must not give them one-word answers, but help them to reflect on what they have seen and done. By this they will learn and grow more mature – someone has described maturity as not making the same mistakes over and over again. If we are to stop that happening, they need to review the first time. I remember a young man coming to me after a New Year party where he knew he had lost control, which was the objective of most people there. By the morning he knew he had done something which he deeply regretted and which, thank God, did not have any permanent consequences. He was so relieved when he knew he was in the clear, but his biggest worry was that he didn't remember anything about what he'd done. After our conversation, he put a strict limit on what he drank at parties as he knew he lost control with too much alcohol inside him – he had learnt and matured the hard way. We must help our young people '. . . grow in the grace and knowledge of our Lord . . . Jesus Christ' (2 Pet. 3:18). Then they will be able to be '. . . shine as lights in the world, holding fast to the word of life' (Phil. 2:15,16).

With our support, teaching and prayers, they should be better equipped.

**THINK AND ACT**

- Take a look at your programme and think of ways you could upgrade your attempts at intentional discipling.

## Books

Tim Hawkins, *Disciples Who Will Last* (Surrey: The Good Book Company, 2002).

# 6.

# A Place to Learn How to Serve as Christians

## A neglected area

You don't read a lot about service in most books about youth ministry. I'm sure it's more important than we think. Youth ministry tends to be so much about what we do *for* the young people – perhaps a result of the concern we have that they might leave, so we have to keep them entertained. In adult church life, once people are settled into our fellowships, we try to give them a role which will make them feel they belong (if they want it), and good relationships are often built with other members of the congregation in working relationships. If it works with adults, why don't we do it with young people? It may well create a greater identity for them with both the youth group and the church. As the church is God's plan for his people to be together, we should not try to create any alternative community. However frustrating (or wonderful!) our church may be, it is God's only way of drawing his people together and we should not try to create an unbiblical alternative. If we are to pass on truths from one generation to the next then all the generations need to acknowledge they are part of *one* community, even if that community meets in age-based or interest groups at sometime during the weekly programme.

Last August I went into church on a weekday morning, and there was a white van parked by the rear door. A large group had been organized to load the van with all the kit that was needed for our youth group's annual week away. Group members were helping to get the gear together, load the van and set everything up in the boarding school they were using. It may sound trivial, but when I did that kind of thing with a youth group I remember watching a guy of 15 walking along the corridor of the school we were staying in, looking at all the labels he had stuck on the doors and feeling very proud of himself. He was part of something, and that sense of belonging is important to us all. I believe it is even more important for young people to feel that sense of belonging than adults. As we have seen, they are living at a time when everything is changing in their world and culture and to feel 'you belong' is very important.

We long for young people to become Christians, and that is at the core of Jesus' call to mission. Our longing must always be to see young people trust Jesus as Lord and Saviour and, once those new babes have been born in Christ, we must help them grow up to be mature believers and acknowledge Jesus as Lord of their lives. But a key lesson in maturity is to believe less and less that you yourself are the centre of your world – to become less ego-centric and more and more Christo-centric. At the heart of our faith is a saviour who rebuked Zebedee's wife when she brought her two boys to Jesus, asking if they could get the two best seats in the kingdom (Matt. 20:20–28). They were more concerned with status than with service.

> But whoever would be great among you must be your servant, and whoever would be the first among you must be your slave, even as the Son of Man came not to be served but to serve, and to give his life as a ransom for many.
> (Matt. 20:26–28)

## Take and *give*

Service is good for a group. The biggest reason of all is that Jesus did it. He is our role model, and he has told us he wants us to do it. If we are learning that service is what God wants from us, we cannot just say to our group 'go out and serve'. We must provide them with service outlets. In doing this, it provides a group activity which draws them together, and they get to know each other in the act of serving. They are learning a vital lesson as they carry out the task. We are the people of God, and we are to serve the God who made us – there are some serious lessons to be learnt about fellowship in the gospel as you weed the church graveyard (Our young people actually did that once or twice!).

I have visited many youth groups over the years, and those that worry me most are the ones where a small and noble band of leaders plan and lead a programme (so far so good). The young people turn up and sit through it, sometimes complain about it, and go home again. That's it! It's a rather nasty form of consumerism where students just take, and give little or nothing – if it doesn't please them, they complain that their leaders are not cool or walk away saying the Christian faith is irrelevant to their lives. You do *not* identify with a group if all you do is *take* – if you contribute, you feel you belong. So what can we do to give opportunities for young people to serve?

Strangely enough, I think this starts with a change of attitude – when I first went into full-time church ministry, I really felt I had to do everything. The room where the group met had to be right and I had to set it up – all the books, Bibles, food, notes, publicity (and much more) was my responsibility. I had to make sure it was all perfect and, if I didn't, I was failing in my duty. In doing so, I had stopped anybody else contributing to the Dave Fenton Show – organized, resourced and delivered by the one and only DF, and nobody else got a look in. They simply turned up and consumed the wonderful 'food' I had prepared. My responsibility, as the church leader responsible for youth ministry, was to make sure it happened, but *not* to do it all. It starts with an understanding of your own gifting – I knew my gifts were largely in the area of teaching and leadership (I hope with humility!), and the wonderful spiritual gift of administration (1 Cor. 12:28) was something God had given to others. The omni-competent automaton that has to do everything and be involved in everything does not appear in Scripture. The leader who stands back, checking that everything is happening, and leaves people to get on with what they've been gifted to do is a biblical leader. It must also be said that if we are truly servants then we all have to do the lowly tasks – standing aloof and saying your only gift is being a visionary would not make you very popular in my teams. I might ask you to roll up your sleeves and help us move the chairs.

We need to understand that the lowly job has to be done, and we all contribute – everyone on the team clears up at the end of an evening or a house party. Nobody leaves until it's all finished. But there are some things that each of us is uniquely gifted to do, and that includes young people. We must look at the way in which we create service opportunities for them. All the examples will either come from things I have done, or ones I have heard about from other leaders.

## In the group

A youth group is a group of God's people gathered together under the leadership of people entrusted with their care. Part of its function is to

> equip the saints for the work of ministry, for building up the body of Christ, until we all attain to the unity of the faith and of the knowledge of the Son of God, to mature manhood
>
> (Eph. 4:12,13)

These verses talk about God giving us spiritual gifts, and God does that to equip us for ministry. Unless you believe that God waits until everyone is 18 years old before he gives out his gifts, those gifts have already been given and must be nurtured and used in the community of faith. You may have someone in your group who loves getting rooms ready for meetings, or enjoys cooking and makes a great pizza. To some people, loading a van or setting up chairs or lighting is a personal joy – there may be others whom God has gifted with a prayer ministry, or who are great at welcoming new people. If you find a teacher in the group, don't just give him a talk to do when most of your leaders are away, work with him on the first five minutes of *your* next talk, and then give encouraging and constructive feedback. If you have some good musicians, then enable them to lead sung worship, but never give them the freedom to do it without feedback. Musicians are notorious for 'going off on one', and often need help to see they are part of the group activity, not an end in themselves. I always try to make musicians contribute somewhere else – they can become elitist in their thinking, and if you sniff anything like that it needs gentle correction. No one gift is more important than any other, and always needs to be seen as building up the whole – that should be taught, as young people often see other people's gifts as a threat, and jealousy can break out. We need to be seen as leaders who acknowledge that all gifts contribute to 'the work of ministry'.

It is difficult to make a long list here – in the previous paragraph I have noted some gifts which I have seen in young people. Take a look at your group and ask yourself if there are young people there whose gifts are not being used, and try to find a way of developing them in your activities.

**THINK AND ACT**

- Make a list of young people in your group – prayerfully think through the gifts you have seen in them and ask yourself where they could be used. A simple table like the one below may help.

| Name | Gifting | Area of Service |
|---|---|---|
| Jo Bloggs | Teacher | Teaching in Sunday school under supervision |
| | | |
| | | |

There are more formal ways of checking out the gifts of young people (e.g. Willow Creek's Network course) – you might also find it helpful to make it a habit to talk to members of your group about how they might be involved. I have sometimes found hidden gifts that way.

But there is something in which all should be involved – praying for one another. With the technology we now have, it is possible to make prayer requests known very quickly. Now that most young people have a mobile phone, it is great to keep in touch with each other during a week in which they may meet only once. They contact each other, but that can create in-groups; you have the technology to contact *everyone* in the group and, the more you do, the more likely it is they will get the inclusive message. My experience suggests that most young people love to contribute to the life of their groups, and want to both feel involved – if you have a purpose for turning up, you probably will.

## Outside the group

Young people spend only a small percentage of their time in their youth group. They are often very busy, involved with all kinds of creative, sporting or leisure activities. But in amongst the range of their activities, they should be encouraged to have some avenue of service. I have seen young people who become involved in too much activity – they go to dancing classes, swimming, and sing in the local opera and that's just on a Monday. They need time to rest and relax without us (or their parents) getting them to do too much. But in the mix of all they do, it's good that at least one thing is *not* about personal pleasure or achievement. Alongside being part of the youth group's activity there may be opportunities in the wider church. Schools sometimes offer a service activity, and involvement in this should be encouraged.

## In church

'We are members together of the body of Christ' – so say all Anglicans in their baptism service, and other churches use similar wording.

> But as it is, God arranged all the members in the body, each one of them, as he chose (1 Cor. 12:18)

I find no biblical reason for excluding young people from that serving community. If they belong, they should be involved in aspects of church life which are appropriate for them. We have two young people sitting on our PCC (the governing group of the church) and they are, therefore, involved in the decisions that need to be made. It is helpful to ask the question, 'What *can't* the young people do?' rather than 'What *can* the young people do?' It was always a joy when, in a church service, a member of the youth group would read the lesson, or pray. With a bit of coaching, they generally did things very well. Some were good at welcoming and most coped with taking the offering – there was even one young man who loved to help count the offering, and he was a bit quicker than some older hands. This is surely the joy of church life. Any opportunity to work across the generations should be grabbed. We saw young people acting as waiters at the senior citizens' Christmas lunch. I have never seen some of them look so smart in their 'waiter uniforms'. I get tired of hearing how bad young people are in our society, and here is a great way to debunk such rubbish and to bring great joy to the older people in your church. If you take a look at your church programme, there will be areas in which young people can be involved.

One key area is work with younger children. This is not just an answer to your staffing problems, but a great opportunity for young people to serve. There are legal issues involved here and they must not be used to boost your ratios of staff to children, but they can be used in creative ways according to their experience. If you run midweek activities, they can be used to help. In our Sunday Explorers group (7s to 11s) young people are leading the singing, being part of a drama presentation, and involved in small-group work. If you have a small youth group, this is a great way for them to feel involved in the life of the church, and in some ways a smaller church has more opportunity for young people to serve. That probably means larger churches have to be keenly aware that young people must be given opportunities in every avenue where service is possible.

There can be dangers! At one extreme we encounter the young person who considers themself the greatest servant of the church since records began, and wants to take over immediately. Then there will be those who feel very insecure and who don't function well. If you are going to use young people, make sure they have received some kind of training and briefing about what you expect of them. I have recently done a training weekend for some of our young people and was impressed with their ability, but also made aware of their need to understand the servant-heartedness of ministry, and to learn from more experienced people. We must never send them into situations and tell them to get on with it. Someone going into a Sunday school situation needs help with

- Simple aims and objectives
- Handling children
- Safety and security
- Appropriate language and touching
- How to lead a small group (see chapter 11)
- How and when to pray with children

Etc.

When I have used young people, I would not send them into a group unless some of those issues had been talked about. It is also helpful to have a more senior leader who can guide and mentor them into good practice. Using young people in church settings just becomes part of the way the church operates. Service linked to training becomes one part of the model of ministry.

## In mission

It is very possible for youth ministry to become very parochial. Many churches have missionary notice boards with pieces of thread connecting the church to a dot on a world map. For youth, there is little personal connection with the people at the end of those threads; those who have gone into foreign fields may get a mention in the weekly bulletin or in church prayers, that's all. When my wife was a missionary correspondent (she wrote regular letters) I remember one missionary not requesting the latest theological tome but a good supply of Agatha Christie novels, and as many pairs of Marks & Spencer tights as were available. These faces on our board are real people who like to curl up for an evening and read a novel, and who miss retail therapy. We must lift up the eyes of our young people from their dangerously self-centred world to see what God is doing. We need to introduce them to the concept of global/local mission. It could start as it did with me; I watched Anneka Rice on the TV when she went to a Romanian orphanage and transformed it in a week. I felt a deep conviction that this was a country I needed to visit. I contacted a Christian agency and they put me in touch with a fledgling Baptist church that needed a partnership with a church in England. That was in 1991, and church members have been going to that same church ever since, never promising to deal with all their issues and thus create dependency, but to do what they can to help in partnership with local believers. The Romanian Christians now say the most important aspect of this relationship is that they keep coming. Summer camps are still staffed by young people from Sheffield.

In the early stages of our connection, young people wrote letters to Romanian teenagers. I regularly took the youth to visit that community, and allowed them to see all aspects of how Romanians lived. When their new church was finally complete, young people went to celebrate with them and our youth group contributed to the salary of the pastor. We made as many 'live' connections as we could – they were people we knew and grew to love, and some of those trans-European friendships have lasted. They were no longer curled up pictures on a church notice board, but real people. In my present church, we have a strong connection with Uganda. A group of young people visited during the summer and were very much involved in school and church work. Such visits leave an indelible mark on their lives. It stops them complaining about how little they have in the UK, and focuses them more on the needs of others. Young people should be given every opportunity to see well beyond the boundaries of their own little world, to see what God is doing in his world. Exposure to another culture and style of ministry has often been the foundation of a call to mission, whether at home or abroad.

**THINK AND ACT**

- Encourage your group to 'adopt' a missionary or mission your church already has a connection with.
- What practical ways could your group develop a partnership with that mission or missionary?

On my computer screen I have a scrappy piece of paper with the phrase

> Mission is NOT crossing the sea, it is seeing the CROSS.

I have no idea who said it, but it reminds me that when young people realize what Christ has done for them, they want to *do something* with their new-found faith.

They are often great enthusiasts who can lack a bit of wisdom but, with the right guidance, they can be greatly used and grow in their faith.

Some people find this a bit daunting – it need not be. It can start with sending Christmas cards to children. The Sunday school leader in Romania gave us the names of all her children, and our Sunday school made cards one Sunday as an activity. If you could see the gratitude at the other end, you wouldn't hesitate. On my first visit to Romania, we took some simple toys to give to children of families in the church – we visited a home one afternoon and gave a boy of about 8 years a simple box of Lego which could be made up to a milk float. As the small plastic pieces came out of the box, the boy stared at them, not knowing what to do. Only when we showed him the plan and how the pieces all fitted together did we see his face light up. He spent the rest of the time we were there taking it apart and assembling it over and over again, and the smile never left his face. I have a picture of that boy which I showed to the child who gave the box of Lego. In the nineties, our children collected 5p coins in Smarties tubes; that paid for an overhead projector (hi-tech in Romania in those days), and we kept all our Sunday school material visual aid pictures and sent them out there. It's not rocket science, but it broadens perspective.

## In community

One last area of service – the community. Down the road from the church in Sheffield were some mill ponds left from the early days of the Industrial Revolution. They were full of rubbish, and the council seemed to believe that if rubbish was under water it was invisible and could be left. One half term, close on the heels of our teaching on Genesis, we tried to help redeem a bit of creation. We removed as much rubbish as the youth group could manage from those ponds. It wasn't a perfect job, but it was an expression of service linked to the teaching programme – it was often cold and wet, but great fun. We do a similar thing at the Keswick Convention every summer when we spend time involved with CAKE (Cleaning Around Keswick Environmentally). We visit gardens to help senior citizens, invite them to tea and go around the town picking up litter.

You may look at this chapter and think you couldn't possibly organize all these things – you're probably right. My examples cover a lot of years of ministry. But I do think that service is a key part of the life of a youth group. We must be careful not to have young people coming to church every hour of the day and night. However, whether you do it with an occasional project or encourage young people to write to a friend for a year, serving is part of what it means to be a Christian. If we tell them about serving Jesus, we have to give them something to do.

# TEACHING AND LEARNING

# 7.

# The Role of the Bible

## Direction needed

My most recent boy's toy, bought for me by my church staff, is a TomTom satellite navigation device. It's great.

I think my colleagues thought I needed one because it gets me right to the door of houses I would have taken hours to find. It even says 'you have reached your destination' when I get there. Our young people are trying to find direction in a world with signposts pointing in a multiplicity of ways. Having negotiated the joy (or otherwise) of childhood, they face the pressures of the teenage years where many voices will be giving them information and guidance about their future. They will move one way or the other by responding to what they think is the most credible advice on offer. They will get advice from somewhere because, at their age, they are looking for ways to live their lives. Their schools will be full of direction, most of it helpful, but not coming from a Judeo-Christian world-view. Of course we must work with our children's schools whenever we can, but be aware that much advice and guidance that is being given here is not based on Christian truth. That is not to say that we should tell our children not to listen to their teachers, but we need to be aware that the school is not concerned with giving our children a world-view that says 'Jesus is Lord' and that God is a loving Father who has plans and purposes for their lives. If we fail to communicate by word and action that God is vitally concerned with all that we do, we have not communicated a biblical gospel. We have left our young people with no Christian world-view map to find their way through life. I have experienced some youth meetings where talks have been full of worthy thoughts and oratory, but they have not communicated a thing about what it means to be a Christian in a twenty-first century world.

> Your word is a lamp to my feet and a light to my path. (Ps. 119:105)

We need to be convinced that when we are teaching the Bible, we are not just engaged in yet another academic exercise. What God has written in his Word is not just designed to titillate our intellect. In the Bible we have stories about people who have tried to follow in the ways of God. That's what we are trying to teach our young people to do. The early story of Abraham (Gen. 12ff.) tells how God guided the man of his choice to the place he wanted him to go.

## Lighting the path

In the world of theatre, you sometimes see a single performer in a small circle of light. The rest of the stage is in total darkness. As the actor moves around the stage, it appears that the small circle of light (created by a 'follow spotlight') is moved by an operator as he follows the actor. Quite the reverse is true. The spotlight operator moves the circle, and the actor is responsible for keeping in the light. The actor steps into the path of the light, otherwise he remains in the dark and cannot be seen by the audience.

Giving 'light to a path' is about how we live our lives – whether we do it blind, in complete darkness, or whether we allow God to light that path with his Word. If the gospel is truly liberating, then it must never be seen or taught as a series of killjoy rules that restrict us from doing everything that is attractive. It must be taught as something which liberates us from the bondage of self-centredness. If we look back to God's plan in creation, we see a beautiful world which is for our joy. It is not for us to tell young people that everything they encounter is full of evil and wickedness. But God did say don't touch the tree of the knowledge of good and evil (see Gen. 2:17) because he wanted his image-created children to learn obedience to the God who had made them the pinnacle of his creation. God had planned a way for his children to live, and he's made that clear in his Word. Our failure to tell young people is a bit like sending them out for a twenty-mile moorland walk in a fog without a map and a compass, and saying, 'See how you get on – you can find your own way, and we're not coming to look for you however long you're missing.'

**THINK AND ACT**

- Think about the times God has spoken to you from his Word.
- Write down some of the verses from the Bible that have been significant at key moments in your life.
- Take time to thank God for speaking to you from his Word.

We should teach with the expectation of life-change. If a young person is convinced that sex before marriage is how it ought to be, then the Bible says otherwise. It limits sexual union to marriage and, if we teach our young people God's precepts, we would hope and pray that their view will be changed. As we teach, the young people begin to assimilate God's wisdom. I once heard a young person say, 'I know it's in the Bible, but I disagree.' If we consistently teach God's Word, that opinion should evaporate as the young people stop seeing the Bible as a book to argue with and begin to see it as a book to be obeyed.

I have been in Christian youth meetings where someone has spoken with great passion and given a very learned message about the text, but never connected with the lives of his audience. The speaker has failed to bring relevance to what is said. I have also sat in meetings where for close on two hours there has been a lot of fun, but God never gets a mention. It was a Christian event but God didn't get an invite. My old boss, Philip Hacking, told a story almost every Christmas about walking along a street and seeing a little boy in tears. He asked him what was wrong and, through many sobs, he explained that he had been so naughty he had been thrown out of his own birthday party. We sometimes do that with our youth meetings; we are so keen to be relevant and 'cool' that we don't like to give God too many mentions, because the kids might get bored. God should be the focus of any event or meeting we run. We are not there to out-gunge the gunge tanks of TV light entertainment. We are there to help our young people live a life of discipleship and grow to maturity. We are reminded to boast in the Bible: 'My soul makes its boast in the LORD; let the humble hear and be glad' (Ps. 34:2).

We want our young people to be so committed to their Lord that they obey him in every aspect of their lives, and boast about Jesus because he is their Saviour and Lord. How can they do that if we tell them very little about him? God has spoken to us through his Word, and our failure to tell young people about the 'glorious deeds of the LORD' (Ps. 78:4) means we have failed to direct their path in ways of godly obedience. Now, of course, our meetings should be attractive, lively and relevant, but don't shut God out by so leading the programme with culturally relevant treacle that God and his Word don't get a look-in. We must teach in such a way that we expect aspects of behaviour to be affected. We must help them understand how to develop and sustain good relationships. To do that they need to understand the true nature of love, and how that works out. The sacrificial love of Jesus points us to how we should love our brothers and sisters. We should apply our teaching in such a way that love is expressed in the relationships within the group.

A booklet published by a local health authority[1] suggests that an orgasm a day is good for you, and gives the following diary as a week in the life of a young person

| | |
|---|---|
| Monday | Five-a-side<br>Ring Alex for time |
| Tuesday | Cinema with Dan and Lucy |
| Wednesday | Masturbate |
| Thursday | Naomi's party<br>Sort out tunes/get condoms/get taxis booked |
| Friday | Date with Sam. Sex! Sex! Sex!<br>Tonight's the night. Bring condoms. |
| Saturday | Lunch at Mum's. Swimming with Matthew and Karen |

The title has a strapline. 'A booklet for workers on why and how to raise the issue of sexual pleasure in sexual health work with young people'. If this kind of material is freely available to our young people, then we need to know to be able to counter such a view of the world.

**THINK AND ACT**

- Talk to your young people about the kind of material available to them.

- Ask them about the conflict they feel between this material and what they believe about living as a Christian.
- You may find they are grateful for the opportunity to talk about it.

## A positive world-view

When such material is openly available to our young people, we are irresponsible if we fail to give some guidance about the world-view that has led to this idea and the consequences of following it.

I have often used the example of walking along the cliffs with one of my grandchildren on a fine but windy day. The wind is offshore and the grandchild is walking perilously close to the cliff edge. I could well say nothing and allow his inquisitive mind to learn the effects of gravity. If a gust catches him and blows him off the edge, he has at least had the chance to experiment with both the force of wind and the acceleration due to gravity. *But he is dead*. The *loving* action would be to warn him of the dangers and, if he persists in walking too near the edge, to tell him to move away, *now*! We may have confused issues of love and discipline, and my observation of the church is that we often fail to encourage young children to live and work within the boundaries the Bible gives us. We are quite happy to preach challenging sermons to our adult congregation, strongly urging them to live godly lives, but in between childhood and adulthood we allow young people the freedom to make up their own mind. We are doing this at the very time where ideas and world-views are being shaped as they listen to other voices craving their attention. The world of popular culture is desperately trying to hook young people into its marketplace, and there are many wholesome areas of creativity in which young people can become involved – but there are plenty which are fraught with danger. We have enough recent examples of people in the music industry who care little about what is reported about them because the oxygen of publicity is their way of life. MTV, the music channel, often speak of their desire to attract 10-year-olds as they consider 14-year-olds to already be devotees of what they transmit.

So there are plenty of ideologies out there, and we must heed the words of Paul if we are to see young people become mature in Christ.

> . . . we may no longer be children, tossed to and fro by the waves and carried about by every wind of doctrine, by human cunning, by craftiness in deceitful schemes. Rather, speaking the truth in love, we are to grow up in every way into him who is the head, into Christ.
>
> (Eph. 4:14,15)

## The way to maturity

Christian maturity will not happen if we simply try to help people engage with culture – we must give them the tools to engage with that culture and help them critique it with discernment. We will not do that unless we teach them what God has said about himself, about his story of salvation, about his gracious dealing with his disobedient people, and about the future hope he has promised us. If we tell them what God has said about himself and his purposes, they will get to know him. I love the game of cricket, and I still enjoy bowling to my grandchildren who are approaching the stage where they can clatter my bowling to the four corners of the local park. I love reading cricket books and I love watching videos of great moments, such as winning the 2005 Ashes series, or Ian Botham's magical innings at Headingly, Leeds, in 1981. If you are not into cricket, you are now totally bored by the last two sentences, but I could go on talking and writing about cricket forever. I will happily engage in conversation with any other cricket fan for as long as they have time to talk. I long for the day when young people in church youth groups up and down the land want to talk on a regular basis about God and learn about what God says in his Word. We must create that appetite by the way we tell them. We must aim for the time when they no longer ask their youth minister what they think, but rather say, 'Will you please teach us what God says in his Word about

Relationships
Money
Family
My boyfriend/girlfriend
The environment
And so on . . .

It's all there in the Bible, and many young people want real answers to the world they live in. If God wrote it, he must want us to take it seriously. Simply to quote a verse and wander off into personal anecdotes, funny stories and extracts from teen magazines, is not teaching young people how to 'grow up into Christ'. One example I heard started well with a quote from the Bible and went a bit like this

- 'Jesus said, "I am the bread of life" (John 6:35).
- Bread is very good for you.

- It's very nourishing.
- We need to be careful what we eat.
- I recently read in a film magazine what the movie stars eat . . .'
- A list of stars and their diets then followed.
- Some quite funny remarks were made about what various movie stars ate, and the effect it had clearly had on them.
- The verse was never mentioned again, nor any other Scripture.
- The next mention of God was the concluding remark, 'God cares about what we eat', and this didn't mean spiritual food.
- The talk was essentially one about following a good dietary regime.

Such teaching can never produce maturity because it says little about God – it tries to appeal to the worldly, but fails to challenge the hearer to a godly life. It doesn't say what the Bible is saying. The Bible does have things to say about how we care for our bodies, but not in John 6:35.

Young people will meet challenges to their values in their schools. At the very least we need to be aware of curriculum areas where, even indirectly, the Christian world-view is being eroded. That has to mean that somewhere our children need to hear what God is saying about how we should live as Christian believers in a predominantly secular world. We could do what schools do – encourage our children on a journey of discovery into all the faiths of the world and hope they conclude that Jesus is the right way. This is sometimes called the 'pick and mix' approach. It's what we used to do in Woolworths at the sweet counter when we personally chose the sweets we liked. But it is not what the Bible tells us to do, and it assumes that young people will make the right choices even though the world they live in is full of competing ideologies. They will meet up with adults who tell them that they are narrow-minded or bigoted if they commit to being a follower of a man who lived over two thousand years ago. We must help them deal with other faiths that claim to be the truth, because their schools are now obliged to be multi-faith communities where each religion is given equal weight. If our Christian young people are to be able to deal with that, they must first know exactly what they believe, and secondly be able to respond to those of other faiths. Peter said in his first epistle

> . . . in your hearts honour Christ the Lord as holy, always being prepared to make a defence to anyone who asks you for a reason for the hope that is in you; yet do it with gentleness and respect
>
> (1 Pet. 3:15)

That is a tough call for young people in their school environments. We are asking them to speak of their faith and to be able to defend it in a classroom where an adult could be attacking the truth they believe. We are also challenged in this verse about how we do it – with gentleness and respect. They do not stand a chance of doing that unless they are equipped. Who would send an army patrol out with no weapons, no leadership and no training? It is setting up our young people to fail if we don't give them some clear understanding of what they believe. We are not in youth ministry to compete with other faiths and hope ours comes out on top. We need the authority of God's Word which is way beyond any authority we might have.

## Read on

It is dangerous to see our teaching sessions as an end in themselves. We should not suggest that all the young people need to do is to sit through our sessions and all will be well. If your teaching is clear and relevant, young people will have a thirst for more. You would hope that if you teach a series on Colossians they will be looking at 1 Thessalonians in their own time. We should long for our youth to become Bible students. If they get an appetite for the reading of Scripture, we have done them a huge favour. If we have also created an approach to Scripture that says, 'I want to know what this passage means because

1. I long to know God better
2. I long to be more devoted to God
3. I long to learn what his will is for my life
4. I am so excited about what God is teaching me'

then we have helped someone to become self-motivated about reading God's Word. Once this happens, you have a maturing disciple on your hands. How exciting is that! So we want them to *read on* for themselves, to be excited and motivated about what they are taught and grow in their love for God and his Word.

## No choice

We need to be totally convinced that God's Word is what it claims to be.

> All scripture is breathed out by God and profitable for teaching, for reproof, for correction, and for training in

> righteousness, that the man of God may be competent, equipped for every good work.
>
> (2 Tim. 3:16)

It is criminally negligent if our youth ministry does not have the teaching of the Bible as its focus and its driver. As youth ministers, we are there to tell the praiseworthy deeds of God in such a way that young people are able to grow more Christ-like and more able to see what is 'of good report' and be able to say, 'choose this day whom you will serve . . . as for me . . . [I] will serve the LORD' (Josh. 24:15).

Joshua also said he meditated on God's Word night and day so he knew who God was, what he was like and what he wanted him to do. How can young people know how to live if all we give them is personal anecdotes and stories? We are in a key place in their lives, and they depend on us for our wealth of experience. But much more, we are their teacher and pastor and sadly there are youth ministers who depend on a personality cult to maintain their credibility. How much better to be known as someone who, for those few years in their formative teenage years, faithfully taught and discipled young people so that, when they left for life in the adult world, they left with an understanding of God's Word that enabled them to keep walking with Christ for the rest of their days. I can think of no higher aim, but it is about the way we tell them. In the following chapters I hope to give you a few training points on how this Bible teaching can be achieved.

**THINK AND ACT**

Reflect on the group meetings you are offering to your young people at the moment.

- How are you helping them critique popular culture?
- Are you teaching the Bible or have your talks become too anecdotal?

This is exciting stuff. God gives us this awesome responsibility to be his voice to young people looking for values and purpose in a world full of religions and ideologies. We preach Christ so that they may know him, grow more like him, and witness for him in a 'crooked and perverse generation, among whom [they will] shine as lights in the world' (Phil. 2:15, NKJV).

# 8.

# The Teacher and Learner

I spent quite a few years teaching mathematics to young people in secondary schools. I tried to make the world of mathematics an exciting place, but not all my students were convinced. At the end of the year, they took an examination which persuaded me that there were some latter-day Einsteins in my class, but there were some who had clearly failed to grasp my gems of teaching. But is teaching the Bible the same as what I used to do with the mystery of mathematics?

## Speaking for God

Charlie Riggs of the Billy Graham Evangelistic Association once said when God speaks through us, we can say more in five minutes with power, conviction and authority, than we could in an hour without God's blessing.[1]

When we speak from God's Word, the dynamic is totally different to what I used to experience in the classroom. I hoped that through my teaching students would become more competent, grow to love the subject, and pass their exams. The dynamic of Bible teaching has very different foundations.

1. We are subject to God's sovereignty.
   We do not teach on the basis of our own knowledge and authority. God wrote his book and we are his servants. We try to speak words which come from him and his Word – we are not peddling our own ideas.
2. There must be a commitment to prayer.
   We are fallible human beings and, as teachers, we can get it horribly wrong. Our prayer is that we speak the truth, the whole truth and nothing but the truth.
3. The Holy Spirit's power is central.
   However dynamic we make our talks, we are neither the power behind what we say or the change agent in young people's lives. The Spirit takes the Word and

introduces us to the Word made flesh (John 1:14). Our job is not to get in the way of what the Spirit would say to the church (Rev. 2; 3)

Long before we get near a group of young people, we need to search our hearts and question our motives. What am I doing when I stand in front of a group and speak to them? What should be the outcome? If God has called you to teach young people, then what you teach them will be a reflection of who you are. Your character and personality will come through in your teaching; this is not just about preparing stunning presentations, but more about reflecting God's Word and character into young lives. So when we get together with our group, we talk about what we are going to learn about God today. We create an expectation that God has got something to say, and wants to say it to us through his Word. We should also be happy to say that we have struggled with this issue (if it's true) and in our teaching make it clear that we are under the authority of God's Word and are very capable of getting it wrong. When I worked in Christ Church Fulwood, Philip Hacking often said in his preaching 'make sure you check out what I'm saying is what God's Word says'. He was not the authority – God's Word was, is, and ever shall be.

**THINK AND ACT**

- Think back over your last few talks. Did you feel that you spoke with conviction?
- What are the things you fiind hardest about delivering a talk to young people?

## Sometimes it's tough work

Nobody pretends it is easy to speak clearly from God's Word. Having examined our motives, we need to be humble about our being entirely dependent on God. We should never become proud or self-congratulatory because if we deliver a powerful message, it is God who is at work. If ever you get to a place where you think you've mastered the art of giving talks, ask God to humble you. As somebody has said, when we speak we are simply one beggar telling another beggar where to get bread. But we must speak with authority and conviction.

> . . . we had boldness in our God to declare to you the gospel of God in the midst of much conflict. For our appeal does not spring from error or impurity or any attempt to deceive, but just as we have been approved by God to be entrusted with the gospel, so we speak, not to please man, but to please God who tests our hearts.
>
> (1 Thess. 2:2-4)

Teachers have been given authority by God to speak his truth, and we are to do it with boldness. Amazingly, God has entrusted us with his wonderful life-saving gospel, so we don't tell them life is all fine, we tell them the gospel. We make it clear that humanity has a problem called sin, Jesus dealt with it on the cross and, if you trust him as Lord and Saviour, your life is secure in him for eternity. So if we follow Jesus we back the winner – the one who has conquered death. I have heard youth speakers tell young people how wonderful Jesus is (and they're right – he is) but fail to tell them about the reality of sin and the reason that Jesus is wonderful – he died to take sin away. We have been approved by God to tell *his gospel*, not an anecdotal tale that we think is more palatable. We speak boldly because it really is a matter of life and death.

## Making true disciples

Our motives must be clear in our own hearts and minds – it is to see our young people become Christians and to grow as Christians. That must be what drives us, rather than any hint of deception, as we are tempted to teach things which are not in God's Word. Some teachers find the idea of warning young people rather offensive. They say that Jesus is all about love so, if Jesus loves them, all they need to do is love him in return. That's true, but it's not the whole story. Let's imagine that you go along to your local park on a cold, frosty morning and the lake has a layer of ice on it. It looks like the perfect place to become the next Torvill and Dean and you skate across the ice to the strains of 'Bolero'. The only trouble is that the ice is only a centimetre thick and will not take your weight. Is it wise to simply say, 'I love skating and I'm sure it will all be fine' or would you have preferred it if someone had put up a sign saying 'Skating is dangerous on this pond'? We might feel the park keeper is a killjoy – but in fact he's a lifesaver. We must turn away from ideas that suggest that discipline is a negative thing. If it is vindictive then it's disastrous and creates resentment. However, teaching young people involves discipline; teaching the Bible is about wanting to create children of God who obey God's commands and walk in his ways. Obedience has been part of the deal since God said to Adam and Eve, 'There's a tree that's off-limits.' You may have noticed the words 'discipline' and 'disciple' are very similar because they are the same root word.

> the Lord disciplines those he loves . . . God disciplines us for our good
>
> (Heb. 12:6,10, NIV)

So sometimes we have to say things that do 'not please men'. We are not trying to create offence or make it difficult for young people to follow Christ. We are trying to please God. We must not become obsessed with dishing out discipline to our young people – it is part of what we do, but not the whole. The scope of teaching is far wider and we must communicate the whole counsel of God in what we teach.

> All Scripture is breathed out by God and profitable for teaching, for reproof, for correction, and for training in righteousness, that the man of God may be competent, equipped for every good work.
>
> (2 Tim. 3:16,17)

## Arranging the food

Our young people need a balanced diet if they are to be like the Christians in Ephesus that Paul wrote to Timothy about. We need teaching so we know about God and who he is and what he has done – we must tell young people about 'the founder and perfecter of our faith' (Heb. 12:2). There is so much to tell, and we will never exhaust all that God has revealed in his Word. But reproof is necessary because we get things wrong and we need to be told. If we never did this to a child, how on earth would they ever learn and be saved from making the same mistake again? Even my youngest grandson (who is only 1 year old) knows he has done something wrong when he grabs the TV remote and starts to chew it. He's a very good little boy, but if he doesn't hear that what he is doing is wrong then his natural inquisitiveness will go on to something else. He has no way of telling he's doing a good or a bad thing unless his parents smile and say 'good boy', or they say with face and voice, 'No – stop it.' Toby needs to be trained to see that some things he gets into are fine, others are not, and some are even dangerous. Our young people need all aspects 2 Timothy 3:16 in our teaching *because* we love them and want to see them shaped by God's Word into men and women of God.

**THINK AND ACT**

- Are you choosing to teach Bible passages which help you avoid the whole counsel of God?
- Are you covering all aspects of 2 Timothy 3:16 in your teaching programme.
- How could you correct any imbalance in your future programme planning?

I don't think there is any book in the Bible we can't teach to young people. It is tempting to stay with the easier or the popular bits but, if we do, we are in danger of constructing our own version of the Bible with all the tough bits cut out. The book of Revelation has twenty-two chapters, not three, and even if the imagery of chapter 4 onwards takes some explaining, it is important to teach through to the end because that gives us the full thrust of what John is trying to say to first-century persecuted believers, and to us. David and Goliath is a great story but the end part of David's life is equally important if we are to understand how God deals with his people. The

Minor Prophets are not off-limits – when I told my team I was hoping to teach the book of Hosea they thought I had lost it, but at the end of it one of the youth group said, 'Can we do Micah next?' That has to be one of the great moments in my ministry.

There are a few simple one-year plans in Appendix 1 which may help you plan your future programmes. Take a look at the balance of what has been covered in the year. Most biblical genres (types of biblical literature) have been touched upon, so your students have been exposed to some of the rich variety of the Scriptures. Hopefully it will whet their appetites for the whole of the book, not just the nice stories.

Two points arise from that young person's request to do more Minor Prophets.

1. God wrote the book – we didn't. God says 'All Scripture is . . . profitable' but dare we be so arrogant that we are tempted to say some bits *aren't* profitable? If we teach only the bits we like, we are telling them about the God we like. If we teach only comfortable words, young people will get the idea 'God is nice' and he never challenges us. Of course we teach that God loves us and encourages us and gives us his power – all of that is true, but it isn't the whole story. There may be times when, because of the way your group is living and behaving, a particular book needs to be taught. But we must never let felt needs be our only guide. I always felt my A-level mathematics students struggled most with the horror of calculus, but I couldn't teach calculus all the time because there were ten other subjects in the syllabus on which there would be examination questions.

   Take a look at the Psalms. One of the great features of the Psalms is praise: 'Oh sing to the LORD a new song; sing to the LORD all the earth!' (Ps. 96:1) But take a look at some other lines from the Psalms.

> Hear a just cause, O LORD; attend to my cry!
> (Ps. 17:1)

> Why, O LORD, do you stand far away?
> Why do you hide yourself in times of trouble?
> (Ps. 10:1)

> O God, you have rejected us, broken our defences;
> you have been angry; oh, restore us.
> (Ps. 60:1)

There are many more which speak of other situations which do not fill the hearts of God's people with praise. If we only teach psalms of praise, our young people will think that in every situation we should be full of praise. That is not my experience. I have experienced times of trouble, and times when God has appeared to be distant and also where I have felt myself to be the victim of injustice. The psalms are full of human emotions and experiences – we give young people the wrong idea if we fail to tell them that God's Word deals with that kind of variety. If they are suffering from the premature death of a parent, or the break-up of their families, there are psalms which express that depth of emotion.

2. My youth wanted more of the same. Learning about Hosea had said to them it was good to learn about the Minor Prophets. What we had taught had stimulated an interest to go on and study more. We only see our young people once or twice a week, and my passion

is that when they get home, they want to look at God's Word for themselves. Our teaching has created a thirst for more. In my teenage years, I was taught mathematics by a delightful fanatic. He loved his subject and expected his students to be totally committed to learning more. I cannot believe I ended up in his home on a Saturday morning with one other student to listen to him go through some new facet of his subject. Any student learns as much in their own study as they do in lectures if they are taking their subject seriously. We must teach in such a way that we create that longing to know more of what God wants to say to us. There is always more to learn – when you've sussed out the Bible, please get in touch and I'll find you a new question to occupy you!

## Creating a thirsty environment

The environment of our group is one where we want to know what God says about himself, the world we live in, the big issues of the day and how we should live. You may be thinking that it would be good if your youth group would sit down for one minute and listen to one word you say, let alone to a talk on the book of Numbers. All your crowd want to do is to jump around and give you grief. I have known that struggle and gone home thinking that most of my words have been wasted because the group were simply not interested. In my experience, locked away in any group are people who do want to learn. If you had the time, you could set up an hour of the week where there is an open invitation to come and join you as you look at what God's Word says. Tell them, 'If you're coming to mess around, then stay away. We still love you and the group will still meet, but we are creating a small group for those who want to learn.' Another way forward is to speak to the leaders of the noisy pack and question their motives for disturbing the group when there are others who want to listen, learn and ask genuine questions. I knew a youth leader who created a smaller group and the noisy crowd could not bear to be excluded from something, so came along and went along with the rules. There ceased to be a need for the sub-group because the environment had been created.

Is this environment all about teaching from the front? Should our youth group meetings simply contain a talk with no chance for comeback? To return to our Cornish Chinese take-away lady – she told us that she had left church as a teenager because she had asked a preacher a question at the end of a service because she had genuinely not understood something. He had told her that it was what everybody believed and she had better accept it like everyone else. There could have been other factors, but her enquiry had been snubbed and there was no way that she could question God's six-foot-above-contradiction preacher. I have met this attitude at all levels of church life. Ministers who claim that their respect is in question if a member of the congregation challenges something they say and youth leaders who tell their group to behave in certain ways because 'they say so'. We know we want to hear teaching that is authoritative, but we do not want teachers who are afraid of dialogue.

In my own church there are many people with questions who have not quite understood what has been said in the pulpit. There have always been young people who don't get it first time round. Should we be surprised if someone has become a Christian from an unchurched background and doesn't yet understand the nature of grace or have a clear working knowledge of the history of the Old Testament? It has been a closed book for the whole of their earthly life; we must not assume they have background knowledge, nor must we assume that they are not capable of absorbing it quickly.

One of my great joys in youth ministry has been working with youth in small groups – a group of three or four, where we can open the Bible and talk about the questions the young people have. Some questions may shock or surprise you, but it gives them the chance, in a secure environment, to talk about their struggles and joys as well as raise the questions about their own understanding of God. We will look at small groups in more detail in chapter 11.

The learning environment of youth ministry needs to be one where the authority of the Word of God is the reference point for all we do. It teaches us about our faith – it instructs us how to live. It tells us the story of God's redemptive plan. A failure to teach it implies that we know better than the sovereign God of the universe who created us for relationship with him. He's taken the trouble to write the book for us, and he knows all there is to know; yet we substitute platitudes, anecdotes and funny stories for God's revelation to the people he created and loves. There's nothing wrong with humour in teaching, but entertainment is not the aim of youth ministry. Most young people have some level of inquisitiveness; if we choose to ignore their questions (however basic we think they are), they will not respond to us. A 15-year-old (who had heard the story in an assembly) came and asked me why Jesus was always on about the vine, and what did it mean. It took me about thirty minutes to go through it, and I've been visited several times since with further questions. Nobody pretends this work is easy – it takes perseverance and time which is very precious to many people. But it is what ministry is about if we are to create mature disciples.

# 9.

# Preparing to Teach

'The one non-negotiable in this church is that we teach the Bible.' That was the phrase I heard many times in my twelve years working with Philip Hacking in Sheffield. Sadly that is not the case in many youth group settings but, as we have already seen, how can we be so cruel as to send our young people into their secular environments ill-equipped and vulnerable? This does not mean that we need to recreate the stereotype of the youth version of the finger-wagging preacher, but it does mean that at some point, someone who is gifted to speak from God's Word and is prepared and ready for it humbly seeks to explain the Word to their group of young people. The learning model we use may differ, but the core principle is that enshrined in this activity is the message God wants to speak to his people, and he uses people like us to do it. We start with

## Key point 1

### *Teaching our young people is the best thing we can do for them*

How we achieve that may differ from place to place, but do it we must – we need to be convinced before we prepare our talks that what we do is of crucial importance to their lives, and therefore deserves the very best we can give. I have seen talks scruffily prepared on the back of envelopes; after all, said one, 'It's only a youth talk.' Of course we must care for them and be there for them in a difficult time, but youth ministry must never become solely relational and deal only with felt needs. If we fail to communicate both the blessings and demands of being a Christian, how on earth will they ever learn how to be a disciple? So often I have heard youth talks which are little more than moral teaching which you can get in years 10 and 11 at school. We must pray for them (and their parents or carers) and we must have fun with them, but at the heart of it must be a passion to share God's Word with them.

People often ask what has kept me going in youth ministry for over forty years, and it is this passion to teach God's Word in a way that young people can understand and will make a difference in their lives. I'm sure you get a lot of newsletters at Christmas where families tell you about the previous year – my best ones are from people who were once in a youth group and are now serving God in their adult lives. So be assured – the finest thing you can do is to teach, even if sometimes it's a struggle and you may doubt your own ability. Most testimonies I have ever heard have a story about someone who took time to teach them.

At this point you may be thinking that you are the Lord's most useless servant. You find teaching hard and the preparation even more taxing and, like all of us, you have to ask if teaching is your gift. It is a spiritual gift (Rom. 12:7), but there are people who find it a real struggle. It should not be likened to academic theology which, of course, has its place; but not every teacher has a degree in theology and you should not beat yourself up because you wish you knew more. If you are someone who loves God's Word and reads it whenever you can, you are excited about what it says and prepared to work hard at preparing the best talks possible, then you are someone who God can use. Remember too that what you are doing is for God, and carried out in the wonderful dynamic of the anointing of the Holy Spirit. You are not alone. We are not trying to be clever or impress people (1 Thess. 2:4), but God has chosen us to do this job for him, and he promises that his Spirit will equip us for the task. That's why you can sometimes do a talk and you're really unhappy about it, but somebody comes up to you afterwards and says it was very helpful.

Many youth ministers lead busy lives and I marvel at many of the people I meet on training courses who somehow manage to cram preparation time into their schedules. But I have never found a short cut method that will save time and help me to produce a great talk in five minutes. If our talk is to mean something it must, first of all, mean everything to us – and we are not in the business of sounding clever. We are in the business of seeing young people's lives change, and must therefore put the work in to prepare well.

## Key point 2

### *Do the best you can with your preparation*

It's very easy to sit and stare at a passage in the Bible and not know what it means, and to have little idea about what you should say about it. You get the feeling that this experience will be like the blind leading the blind. Where do you start?

Your initial questions might be

- Who was the author?
- Where was he when he wrote it?
- Who were his first readers, and what do we know about them?
- What did this piece of writing have to say to those people?

It's no different to how we would treat a modern historical event. If you simply said, 'There were many soldiers on a French beach' it fails to give the reality of what was happening on D-Day. Why were the soldiers there? Why were they being shot at? Why was there a war on? And so on. Yet so often we fail to give our young people the context of the passage we are teaching. Why were the children of Israel standing with their backs to the Red Sea with Egyptian chariots rapidly approaching? That situation needs a context or it can appear rather bizarre. Why was the prophet Hosea asked by God to 'Go, take to yourself a wife of whoredom and have children of whoredom' (Hos. 1:2). We need to say more than 'What an interesting new insight into choosing your partner for life!' and ask what God's purpose was in saying that to Hosea. Hosea is a great book to teach to young people, but not without understanding its context – it will make no sense.

I have a danger that I will spend too much time looking in this area because I am fascinated by the background in terms of political and military issues. I have to be careful that I don't get carried away – but some background is vital. If you were teaching the period in Exodus where the children of Israel were in Egyptian bondage, then there are some great pictures around on the Internet of what the buildings and palaces looked like in Egypt. You don't necessarily tell your young people everything you know, but thirty minutes in a Study Bible or Bible handbook can yield a rich reward and be a great blessing to your group. Three minutes of background can paint a picture to stimulate them to find out more for themselves, and also enables you to teach in a way which has meaning.

It's also good to find out a little about the writer and what he was like. Amos was not shy when it came to some of his public proclamations: 'I hate, I despise your feasts, and I take no delight in your solemn assemblies' (Amos 5:21). It's very easy to look at that and think Amos was the biggest whinger who ever walked on the earth – unless you realize that at the time, the people of Israel were enjoying prosperity, treating it as a sign of God's blessing yet failing to acknowledge God as the giver of all good things. This southern kingdom prophet was told by God to go to the northern kingdom of Israel and warn them about living in prosperity when many of their people were poor and downtrodden. Amos is the great prophet of God's justice, and he told Israel that their prosperity had been achieved at the expense of their citizens. A short look at the situation in Israel at the time brings the book of Amos to life.

My previous two examples have both been from the Minor Prophets, and my choice is deliberate. We often ignore these books because we find their words or their images too hard to handle. But it doesn't take long to bring a book to life if you spend time trying to understand what's going on.

## Key point 3

### *What kind of book is this?*

Many people take a book on holiday – it helps us go to sleep on the beach. We may have to a read a technical book as part of our daily work, and it's important we understand it if we are to do our work well. We may have books in our lounge which remind us of a happy holiday in the mountains of Scotland. Not all books have the same function, nor are they written in the same style. You wouldn't read your book of mountain pictures to tell you how to make your television work, so we must treat each book in the way its genre demands. If we fail to understand this we will make a book of the Bible say something different to its key purpose. You can find different titles in reference books for the categories but they fit quite well into these:

- History (Exodus or Acts)
- Prophecy (Isaiah, Hosea or Amos)
- Wisdom (Ecclesiastes or Proverbs)
- Poetry (Psalms)
- Gospels (Matthew or John)

- Epistles (Colossians or 1 Peter)
- Apocalyptic (Daniel or Revelation)

**THINK AND ACT**

- Make a list of the books of the Bible and allocate them to one of the different genres above. That may not be as simple as it sounds – some books contain writing in more than one genre.

'Apocalyptic' has often been a word that frightens people away from a book which has much to teach us. Revelation was written at a time when persecution was growing in the church, and God wanted to convince his people that despite what was happening to them, all would be well. God could be trusted and Satan would be defeated – *fear not*. That message was stark and much needed in the late first century – and needs to be heard in our modern world. It is usually the imagery that frightens us, but if you approach Revelation chapter by chapter, you will see what the slightly strange images mean and how relevant they are for us today.

**THINK AND ACT**

- Choose a book of the Bible (preferably one you are not too familiar with e.g. Lamentations of Nahum.
- Using a Study Bible or a Bible handbook, try to find out as much as you can about the background to that book.

So the way we deal with an apocalyptic book is different to the way we look at Exodus; the questions we ask of the book will be different. With Exodus, we can use some evidence from archaeology which tells us there were Egyptian palaces and there was a city called Jericho which God (through Joshua and his friends) flattened the walls of. But we shouldn't treat Revelation the same way and see if we can dig up 'the burning lake of fire'. Many people have got into trouble because they fail to distinguish between the metaphor and what is real historical fact.

If we know something about the people and places involved, then we stand a chance of finding out what the passage means. We must avoid making jumps that the Bible doesn't want us to make. Having read the story of Jesus washing the feet of his disciples, it is unlikely we should all remove our socks and shoes and ask our church leader to visit the youth group and wash everyone's feet.

## Key Point 4

### *What does it mean?*

We have to be careful with this area, because if we get this wrong we can miss the message that God has for us. Not everybody killed giants in the story of David and Goliath. Only David did that. The rest of the people of Israel were stood on a hillside quaking in their boots until the giant lay dead and their courage (or maybe their trust in God) returned. So it is unlikely that the meaning of that piece of historical narrative is there to teach us that we can slay giants in our lives just like David. In that context (about a thousand years before

Jesus), the people of Israel were on the rack as the Philistines constantly made a nuisance of themselves. Israel needed a saviour, and an extremely unlikely answer was a shepherd boy who had come with his brothers' lunch and ended up facing an aggressive oversized Philistine. God had provided a saviour who, because he trusted that God had authority over everything on the planet, could certainly deal with a loudmouth from the coast. Of course this points us to Jesus, but then the Old Testament does that on every page, and that's one aspect of a story we should always be looking for. If we can trust God to deliver his people in the Valley of Elah over three thousand years ago, we know he will deliver us from sin – and only Jesus, by his death on the cross, can deliver us from sin's shackles.

You may have noticed that as I tried to dig out the meaning of that story, there were little bits of background which popped up as the story was told. Every talk does not need to be neatly defined as five minutes on context, followed by five minutes on meaning, and driving home the application at the end.

It may help you to ask some other questions in trying to establish the meaning of the passage. Don't give up too easily on this and remember that the Bible is not just a book for scholars. It's God's Word for all humankind; we must never allow the Bible to drift into the realm of an academic text book – it isn't. If we fail to understand the meaning for the original hearers, we may put our own twenty-first century meaning on a passage which could lead us astray. What did it mean to the residents of Philippi when Paul told them they were 'citizens of heaven' (Phil. 3:20, NLT). Some of the proudest people in the New Testament were the Philippians, who had been granted the same level of citizenship as the residents of Rome itself even though they lived miles away from it.

What really matters, says Paul, is that we need to be people who are citizens of the kingdom of God, which God is drawing to himself as men and women who trust in Christ. That is infinitely more important than the fact that you live in Philippi. The meaning of that phrase comes from an understanding of the context.

You may need to ask

- What is the main thrust of this passage – don't look for peripheral meanings, look at the big message. That is probably what you want your young people to go home with.
- Is this idea anywhere else in Scripture, and do I need to use that other scripture to help me be clear about this teaching? If you are teaching on dealing with suffering, I would want to look at several passages before I taught that lesson from one.
- What does this passage teach me about God, Jesus and the Holy Spirit? The key application is probably to be found in the answer to this question.
- For your own good, it is always important to ask, what does this passage tell me about *me*? If we learn a lesson from it, it will help us tell the young people some things that will help them live lives that please God

## Key Point 5

### *What does it mean for me?*

It is very rare when you teach that it does not leave people with a question about their own life. Inevitably, when we teach people about God, what he's done and how we should live, it raises questions. If you teach 'love your enemies' that will raise issues for many young people. How do you love the student at school who bullies you, or gives you a hard time for being a Christian? But let the Bible do the talking. Don't allow yourself to use the Bible to say something you feel passionate about at the time. Many of us want to jump to the meaning a bit too quickly. We can easily leap in the wrong direction, but we must aim to leave our young people with at least one point of application. Our talks are not academic walks through the Scriptures – they are life-changers and, as God's Holy Spirit works in people's lives (remember, it's he who does the changing, not you) it could mean that young people could be very encouraged or deeply challenged. Pete Ward (at the time, the Archbishop of Canterbury's Youth Adviser) said in an interview that his experience had taught him that there were thousands of young people miles away from the culture of most church-based youth groups. Whatever one did, he said, he believed one could not reach 70 per cent of the young people living in the UK.[1]

In saying this, Ward implies that the Bible cannot be effective in the lives of the majority of the youth population. I do not believe we can place a limit like that on God's power in speaking through his Word.

When Paul was in jail in Philippi with his mate Silas and singing his version of *Hymns Ancient and Modern*, there was an earthquake. The whole building opened up and Paul and Silas walked out, but the jailer would have been in deep trouble. He was about to take his own life when Paul talked to him about Jesus, and he repented and trusted Jesus as his Saviour; Paul saw wonderful life transformation happen in the jailer's house. That is not exactly an everyday occurrence in my life, so what has it got to do with me? The application is clearly not that the next time you are sat in a first-century jail, sing some hymns and you'll be out of there in a flash. Having understood the meaning of what happened, the application is that in any situation God is with us, however dire that may be. And, because God is in control, he can bring good out of that situation. Then we can start talking about how that applies in the lives of young people.

One of our youth team at the Keswick Convention went swimming in one of the beautiful lakes, was taken ill and died. It was a huge tragedy for us as a team, but massive for his family. You cannot minimize the tragedy of that event, but many of his family and friends were deeply impacted by his death and, when they read his diary, they realized that he had been praying for all of them for many months. A dire situation had led to many people being impacted by the gospel.

It is always good to speak about the situations your young people will meet. One of my group was once faced with an extremely aggressive anti-Christian teacher in a sixth-form class. He never won any arguments with this articulate atheist, but some of his fellow students became interested in the gospel because of the gracious way he dealt with that unprofessional attack by the teacher.

It may not always be an obvious link to an everyday situation that makes up your application. It may not be an action point, but something to go away and think about. *Is* my attitude to the opposite sex how it should be, having seen the way in which Boaz dealt with Ruth? Do I need to think through the way I treat my girlfriend? Having looked at the creation story and understood how we are to look after the world God made, do I need to rethink my attitude to environmental issues?

It may be that having seen the way Jesus had compassion on those he met, we need to have a softer heart – a change of attitude towards those around us. Perhaps we can so easily drift into legalism, or maybe we've allowed jealousy to bite very deep. We need a change of heart. Taking that a little further, we need to apologize to someone (maybe our parents) for the way we've treated them. So the change of heart leads to action. Or it could be that we have a habit which needs dealing with. We are addicted to computer games and we get very stubborn when that is challenged. If that is so, then God is asking us to bend our stubborn wills to his ways.

As you work through the applications of a passage, don't make the passage say what you want it to say. All of us have things we feel passionately about, and we must be disciplined so that we don't constantly thrust our agenda on the young people and make every passage in the Bible say that we all ought to be missionaries in Africa. So we prepare humbly before God, asking him, as we pray for his leading, to speak words of truth that will be transforming. We give as much time as we realistically can to prepare talks. Maybe it's hard for you to create the time for this work, and all you can do is pull a prepared session from a book. Phil Moon addresses this issue in *Young People and the Bible* when he talks about the 'creative ladder'

> At the bottom end, people are totally dependent on published resource. They plug into these and follow every detail . . . At the top end, people don't use any published resources; they start with a blank sheet of paper, dream up scintillating games and activities without any difficulty[2]

Very few of us can produce brilliant sessions week in and week out, but we should strive to gradually move up Phil's creative ladder as we try to do our own research and learn what God's Word says. In the next chapter we will take a look at putting a whole session together.

**THINK AND ACT**

- When you have a spare thirty minues (and somebody has bought you a study Bible for your birthday), choose a book from the Bible that you know very little about.

YOU ARE NOT PREPARING A TALK
Find out as much as you can about that book.

- Who wrote it?
- Who were the big powers around at the time?
- Who is the central character?
- What is the key thrust in the meaning of the book?
- Write down three things the book teaches you about God.
- Write down a lesson you need to learn from the book.

Repeat in a month's time – it will take you about five years to cover every book of the Bible.

## Books

Vaughan Roberts, *God's Big Picture* (Nottingham: IVP, 2004).
Tim Chester, *From Creation to New Creation* (Surrey: The Good Book Company, 2010).

# 10.

# A Worked Example

So far we've looked at understanding the passage or doctrine we are teaching, and how we develop our understanding of it. We've looked at preparing our-selves for the role God has called us to – to faithfully teach his Word. But it is 11:30 on Saturday night and we will be facing a group in the morning, and we know we are not ready for that challenge. Somehow the previous week has crowded in on us and preparation time has been in very short supply. Many youth leaders I know feel this pressure, and this chapter is designed to help you be well prepared for the time with your youth group. Needless to say, it is best to be preparing before 11:30 on Saturday night. What that lateness cuts out is the time you spend thinking about what you will be teaching so that it is more than a list of facts and ideas that you have hastily scribbled down. It is something that is part of you – that God has given to you to pass on. God is quite capable of working in you until any hour of the night, but he does encourage us to spend time meditating on his Word: 'Oh how I love your law! It is my mediation all the day' (Ps. 119: 97). You may think 'all the day' is a bit hard to do, but if you have started your prep and you have some rough notes in your briefcase as you journey to work, your forty-five minutes on the train gives you an opportunity to both scribble down some more thoughts, and to think about what you are going to teach. I travel to London from my home in Southampton on a regular basis. I often use that precious time to either gaze out of the window (also good for you!) or to think about what I have to teach on Sunday.

**THINK AND ACT**

- Look at Psalm 119 (yes, all of it) to see what the writer thinks of God's Word.
- Write down all the attributes that he describes, e.g. 'I love your law'.

- Pray that God will help you have the same attitude to his word as the psalmist.

This chapter is going to feel a bit like *my talk/your talk*. I will take you through from the start of preparing a session and encourage you to do the same with yours, but with different Bible verses. My story is Jesus' parable of the workers in the vineyard (Matt. 20:1-16). The first thing to do is to read the passage and try to understand it.

## STAGE 1 – read the passage three times

When you read it, you may see the story as Jesus' comment on industrial relations or employment law. It does seem a little unfair (as we see it) for someone to turn up in time for tea and for him to be paid the same amount as someone who works through the heat of a whole day for the same wages. This parable raises questions about fairness and justice, and it can make Jesus out to be unfair. Whatever does he mean in the crunch line at the end – 'the last will be first, and the first will be last'? That sounds like you can roll out of bed at noon, have a restful lunch, turn up for work as it gets cooler, and end up with as much cash as the person who's worked all day. Offices and factories would not survive long on that basis, so clearly we haven't found the purpose behind Jesus' parable.

## STAGE 2 – sort out the key points of the story

I like to write down the key points of any passage to make sure I have the order and the detail right. This is easiest done with a series of bullet points. These are mine for this story, but you may well want to refine them. You may think some of them are very obvious but it helps to have them all down.

- This story is told by Jesus.
- He is teaching us about the kingdom of God – the kingdom he instituted when he came to earth and which one day will be completely established in heaven. This kingdom is about our relationship with Jesus. It has no earthly 'land'. It is within the hearts of his people.
- The master goes out early in the morning to look for those who will work for him. That would more likely be done by a senior member of the house, or a trusted servant. The hirer would go into the marketplace where there would be many people saying, 'Give us a job.'
- The master owns a vineyard – the vine was the symbol of God's people. It was carved over the entrance of a gate in Jerusalem. The vineyard is the place for God's people, and the master has gone out looking for people to come there.
- He agrees a wage for the day with the first workers – a denarius was a good wage. It was what a Roman centurion got for a day's work. The wage was both agreed and generous. Not all workers got that much.
- The first workers are sent into the vineyard. The owner sends them. It is assumed they went in happy. They had work and the promise of generous payment.
- The master goes out again at the third hour (about 9:00 a.m.) – hours ran from six in the morning to six in the evening. These workers weren't doing anything useful. They were standing around.

- The master hires them on *his terms* – 'whatever is right I will give you.' Clearly the master decides what is right.
- He repeats the hiring process at noon and at three in the afternoon.
- Finally he goes out again at 5:00 p.m. (only an hour to go) and finds workers who have been idle all day. This would have been unheard of at the time. Those men would not have believed their luck. But the master hires them and sends them into the vineyard (by implication – to do something worthwhile even it is only for one hour).
- The workers say it is because no one has hired them. They have been rejected all day, but at the eleventh hour they are called by the master
- Crunch time! All of those who have been hired at different times are called into the presence of the master. In our money it should have been £12 for the first lot, and £1 for those hired at 5:00 p.m. That's fair – surely!
- One by one they are paid – the 5:00 p.m. crew get the denarius (a good day's wage) for one hour of work.
- It's only then they start to complain. If the one hour man gets £12, then we should get £144 because we've done twelve times the amount of work – 'they thought they would receive more' even though they have agreed a good wage with the master and were happy with it. They get specific: 'We've worked all day and you chose us first. This rabble you got at five was the riff-raff that was left and nobody wanted until you picked them up!'
- The master responds. He says he has done nothing wrong. 'You have been paid what we agreed. You may have what belongs to you because I made a promise and I have kept it.'
- The master chooses what he will give – he is the master and he is generous. Not a single worker is

short-changed. Everyone gets (at the very least) what he promised – some get more than they deserve. He is the sole arbiter of the blessings each person gets, but his blessings are more than generous – 'do you begrudge my generosity', he says. To put it simply, 'Are you turning up your nose at what I've given you?'

- The master says his priorities are not the usual ones – the first will be last and vice versa, and we had better get used to his values. He is the giver. God invites all into his kingdom, and the reward is his blessing.

**THINK AND ACT**

- My suggestion for your story is two chapters earlier in Matthew's gospel – chapter 18:21–35). Choose something else if you want to.
- Notice it's another 'kingdom' parable, so there may be parallels with Matthew 20.
- Read the story three times and write down the key points. If you don't understand the background, try to find out about it (e.g. what is 10,000 talents in today's money – it may change the emphasis).
- Carry your 'key points' piece of paper around with you if you can, so you can jot things down when they come into your head (a good general principle).

I hope that gives you both the thread of the story Jesus tells and some of the background we can so easily miss. For example, the vine is such a potent image in Israel that all his first-century hearers would have been very attentive at that point. 'What is this teacher going to say about the state of God's people? Doesn't he know we've got Romans garrisoned all over our land that God has promised us?' But Jesus says my kingdom is not about land – it's about the heart and your love for God and your devotion to him. This is a very different kingdom not judged on 'worldly fairness'.

This early preparation work is hard but essential if you are going to teach what the parable says. Somebody did tell me he had heard this preached and the speaker rounded off his talk by saying, 'Jesus hates trade unions and all employment law should be torn up.' That kind of nonsense would not happen if that preacher had taken the trouble to understand the background to the story.

## STAGE 3 – Write your notes

You are now writing the story in note form to tell to your group. Your notes need to be legible and help you rather than hinder you. I try always to have notes to which I can return to after I have made eye contact with the group. Some people use highlighter pens to bring out key points, but I would not attempt to give any talk without notes. You can only do it if you have an exceptional memory. At some point in your talk there needs to be some attempt to teach the passage, to extract its meaning, and then some point(s) of application. After you have written your notes, ask yourself how this can best be delivered. Would it be most effective at the end of your meeting? Does it work in three parts, with group times after each part? You are now at the stage where you want to see how the whole learning experience is going to be built around the passage you are teaching.

Your question is always 'How best can I design this meeting in order that the young people will hear God speak from his Word?

## STAGE 4 – Build a session

Keeping in mind that key objective from the previous paragraph ('How will young people hear God speak?'), you must now build into your programme items which will enhance that objective, not detract from it. If I am responsible for a meeting, I carry around an A4 sheet of paper split up into random boxes.

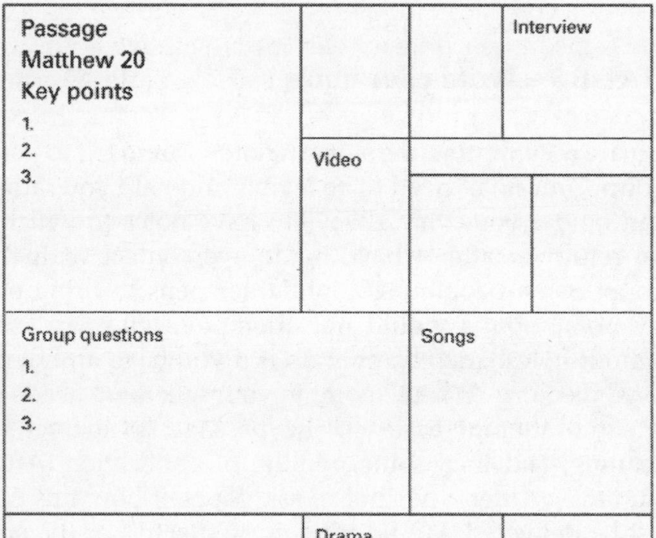

Passage
Matthew 20
Key points
1.
2.
3.

Interview

Video

Group questions
1.
2.
3.

Songs

Drama

In the main box (top left) are the key points to be taught in that session, so those sit there as a reminder of what is to be added. You may have a perfect memory, but I have been known to have a good idea and then forget it completely. So I carry this sheet around so that, if a flash of rare genius occurs, I write it in one of the boxes. The reason the boxes are random is that I am not, at this stage, interested in which order they come in – I am only interested in the fact that it will help our session. There are all kinds of things which might appear in these boxes.

- A song that would fit perfectly with the theme and we could sing after the talk.
- A video clip from a TV soap or a news programme which illustrates one of the points from the talk and gives a contemporary and applied feel to the session.
- A game in which the objective fits with what you are trying to teach – games, for their own sake or as an icebreaker, need to be geared to the learning.
- An interview with a member of your church who has faced the issues you are dealing with.
- A drama sketch using group members – brief them on the theme and ask them to come up with something. Check it out before they perform it.
- What are the key things you need to tell the group (the notices!). Are they best done at the beginning or the end?
- A set of three songs which set the scene for the talk or group time(s).
- Etc.

Let your creativity loose, and use the gifts of your team and the young people to put together ideas which may be useful. Your team may have seen and heard different things and have insights which have never crossed your mind. One of the great joys of ministry is working in teams where people contribute ideas. As members grow in their trust for each other, you are able to put together some high quality sessions which are the product of many minds.

By now you should have a sheet of paper with lots of ideas.

**THINK AND ACT**

- If you have a team of people it can be a great training exercise to give every team member a sheet prior to your next leaders' meeting.
- When you meet together, brainstorm all your ideas into the 'best ideas' for your session.
- Look again at your story (Matt. 18:21–35) and think of programme items which will fit around your teaching.

## STAGE 5 – Running order

We should, by now, have all the elements of our programme in place. It is easy to think you have sorted it all out. But you haven't. The order in which things occur in a programme is of vital importance. You need to look at the changes in the intensity of your programme elements. A lot of this is common sense – you wouldn't announce that a group member is seriously ill in hospital in between two rousing praise songs. It just doesn't fit. Creating atmosphere should never be overdone, but it is something that may make your sessions easier. For example if you sing a quieter song, follow it with a prayer, the mood is quieter for the speaker to begin their talk. Trying to get quiet just after you announce two leaders have just got engaged may be hard work (I actually saw that happen and the young people did not listen to the first five minutes of the talk – they were buzzing).

Once you have the order, write it down so that all contributors know what's coming. It is preferable to time each element, but often hard to keep to the schedule. If you want the whole thing to run smoothly, it is essential for every contributor to know what's happening and when. This way you avoid those embarrassing moments where the team all stare at each other wondering whose go it is next. We do not want to appear embarrassingly slick, but if we feel the job of communicating God's truth is worth doing, then we should give the impression that we have given our sessions time and thought.

A simple running order might be (the numbers are time in minutes)

- Welcome (1)
- Prayer by a young person (2)
- Speaker introduces the topic (1)
- Group time 1 to begin to think about the topic that the leader has opened up (10)
- Key notices – all notice-givers be ready at the front (5)
- Sung worship (x3) (10)
- Talk 1 (7)
- Group time 2 (8)
- Relevant game/activity (5)
- Talk 2 (8) + prayer time (10)
- Final song (3)

That is sixty-two minutes, but you may find things overrun a little if someone does not keep things moving.

This may all seem a little mundane, but I have witnessed too many badly run youth meetings not to be concerned that they can be run better. They need to have warmth so that the young people feel welcomed and accepted. But the youth also need to leave having been encouraged to 'live lives worthy of God' (1 Thess. 2:12, NIV). There needs to be a sense of excitement that we are doing something worth doing. I am not suggesting that you should follow my structures precisely. But the principle remains – good sessions are not done from the back of an envelope. They need to be well thought-out and carefully planned. It is always worth working from the teaching section of your session, and building everything around that central aim. If your group is smaller, you may be able to teach in a more interactive style, but your talk still needs to be prepared and the questions you use need to be as well. Some people try to lead small groups without any preparation.

## Stages 1 to 5 – pray

Having prepared as well as you can, you come to the point where the session is about to begin and you have to deliver it. But you are not giving a lecture or a seminar – you are speaking for God. Some of the young people may not want to hear what you say – some may be resistant. It is vital to realize at this point that any growth in young lives that happens is not down to you. It is God who is the one who changes lives. Our responsibility is to be as carefully prepared as we can be so that God can use us. If this is to happen we must pray from the start of the process to the end. Pray before you ever touch the Bible or your notebook that God will give you wisdom and understanding as you prepare. Pray for good illustrations in your talk and so on – God has promised to give us all the wisdom we need.

Try to make sure you get there before the time of your group meeting. You need to be sure everything is in place, and once it is, leave enough time to pray together. It's good to create the culture which says that all the leaders and young people taking part turn up to pray, to ask God to bless the session and all the young people who come. We want to see God move in the lives of our young people.

> And he told them a parable to the effect that they ought always to pray and not lose heart.
>
> (Luke 18:1)

If you pray, you can keep going. If you don't, you'll want to give in.

# 11.

# Small Groups Mean Larger Groups

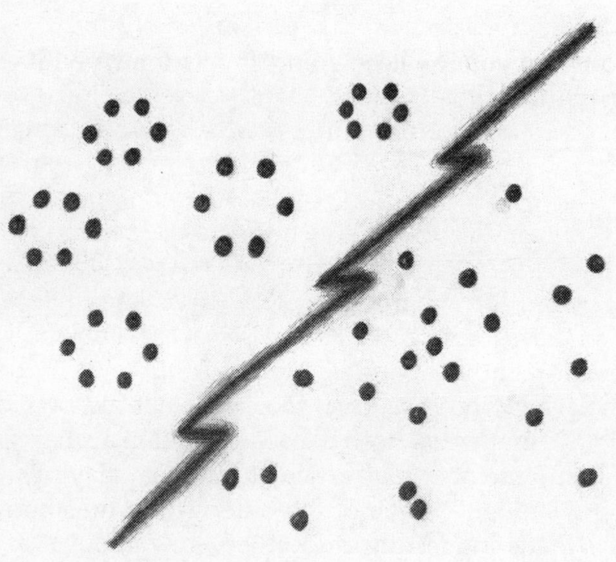

I seriously wondered about putting anything into this book about working in small groups. What clinched it for me was two-fold.

1. It's probably the thing that most youth workers do. After the talk (given by one person) the young people are told to 'go into groups' and most (if not all) of the team will be involved.
2. It's the thing that many people find the hardest. If the group experiences long silences, it can make it feel as if things aren't going well – it certainly doesn't feel like a positive learning experience.
   Small groups – why?

You may often have asked that question. Wouldn't it just be easier to teach the passage and send them home? It may be easier, but would it be better? What do we gain by using small groups in our ministry? Is it not just a sharing of ignorance? The idea of 'peer groups' is fashionable in some places. I have no problem with young people meeting up with each other to share ideas or pray together. But if groups are to be used as a learning environment, there has to be somebody there to learn from. Young people are very capable of jumping to wrong conclusions and need some guidance towards truth. It really depends on what we want them to strive for. If it is to find out what their friends think the Bible means then they don't need a leader to guide them – they may get the right idea, but they may not. If we want them to find what God says, then the consistent message of the Bible is that we *all* need a teacher, even in a small group. A group member may articulate an idea, may say something strange – some of the other group members may say 'that's interesting' and others may adopt it as their idea too. A wrong idea has been planted into young minds and that has to be bad news.

On the other hand, if young people have listened to a great talk but found some ideas hard to grasp, we need to create a place where honest questions can be asked. They may have misunderstood, and the small group gives the opportunity to listen to the issues they will face. 'Love your enemies' could open up a discussion on what love means, what we mean by an 'enemy', or how we apply that at school at 9:00 a.m. on Monday morning. A small group, if handled sensitively, gives young people a chance to express their doubts. Not every young person sits through our talks and believes and accepts every word we say. They sometimes think 'Is that really true?' and need a place for clarification. It may challenge something they have heard at school, and the two ideas may be in conflict with each other. In my research for my writing about 'prodigal' young people, I came across a 17-year-old who said all his youth minister would say to him was, 'It's in the Bible, so believe it.' He left his church and youth group because nobody would sit down with him and help him understand the truth. He was rather sad when he told me he had found an atheistic college tutor who gladly sat with him and helped him. His current view is that Christians are dogmatic non-listeners, and atheists are quite sensitive and good listeners. I hope that view changes soon.

The small group gives us opportunities both to get to know a smaller number of young people more deeply and to understand a little better what they are thinking. If we listen carefully it may encourage us to change the way we teach because we may not be making it clear what the Bible teaches.

## Small groups – when?

We have already talked in chapter 5 about using one-to-ones and small discipleship groups. We now want to look at how we use the smaller group in a teaching session. My experience of churches up and down the land is that small groups are used at a particular time – after the talk. The teacher does his talk and then says, 'Let's go into groups and talk about this.' Youth group meetings can become predictable; we know it happens every week because it always has. *Teach* then *groups* is what you do.

**THINK AND ACT**

- Look back at your youth group meetings over the past two months.
- Did you use small groups every week?
- Were they always at the same time?
- When did your leaders get the questions to be used in the group discussion?
- Did they get any at all?
- Did the groups go well – have you asked?

There are other ways of using groups. I once did a series on the Ten Commandments and, rather than teach the commandment and then ask the young people to decide in their groups whether they were obeying it, I started the whole session with a statement such as

> Today, we are looking at what it means to honour your father and mother.
> Do you – and what does 'honour' mean?

They looked a little startled – you could sense the non-verbal communication. The reason I did it was, before I taught what the Bible said about mums and dads, I wanted them to be real about how they treated their parents. I didn't want them to get the ideal version first. That could easily close up their small group because, having heard what they *should* do, they would be reluctant to talk about what they *really* do. In other words, a small group, at the beginning, opens up the issue in their world and creates a realization that God has a better way when they hear the teaching. But don't do it every week. Use small groups in a way that's going to give the most benefit in understanding the meaning.

There could be occasions where it would be unhelpful to use small groups. If you have taught about the wonder and majesty of God's creation, the last thing you want is a debate about Richard Dawkins (that may come later) or whether microbiology or astronomy best expresses the creative power of God. What you need is to lead the group into worship where they can express the wonder you have tried to teach them about. Again it is the learning objective of the whole session which tells you if and when to use small groups. The traditional way (and sometimes the best) is to follow a talk with questions to discuss which focus on the key ideas of that passage. But there may be a time where there three short talks, each of which is followed by a shorter, more focused time in small groups. I once taught the story of Naboth's Vineyard (1 Kgs. 21). We used a T1G1 T2G2 T3G3 structure ('T' stands for 'teach', 'G' stands for 'group'), where I taught some of the background, followed by a group time; then I taught the narrative and we researched that in groups. Then we had a third group time looking at the application of the story. Again the question is always, how are the young people going to best understand the story, its meaning and its application? Use small groups to assist that process.

## Working with a group

Many people do not find this easy. Their youth group seem reluctant to respond, and there are often those who talk too much and dominate a group time. When we get nervous or we are anxious that the group isn't going well, it is easy for a group time to turn into another talk. We talk too much because we feel the need to fill in the gaps of silence.

### THINK AND ACT

- If you are in a team (two counts as a team), share your recent experiences of leading small groups.
- Has it been a rewarding experience?
- What kind of people do you find it hard to deal with?
- How do you cope with long pauses?

Perhaps the initial set-up of the group needs a bit of attention. A few basic points about set-up should get the group off to a good start.

There are at least three things at work in any small group situation.

1. **Task**
   There is always a task to be completed. Get through a Bible study, and so on. But if we focus only on getting through the work, we will fail to spot how the group is getting on. Is what we are doing creating good relationships, or is it destroying them because all you seem to care about is getting through the questions?

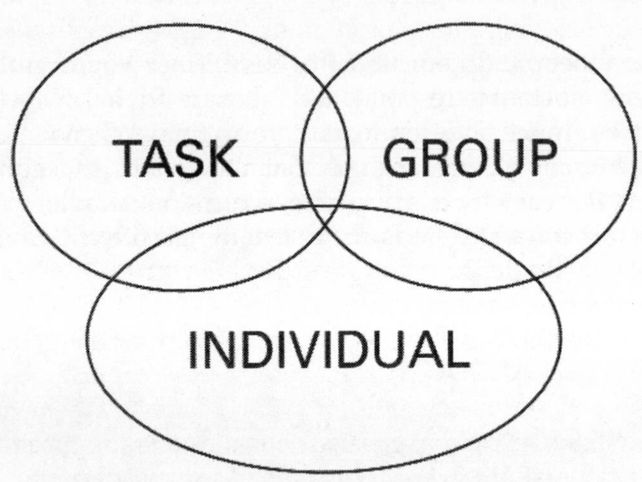


2. **Group**
   Group times are a great way to build relationships, and develop an ability to learn respect for each other. A leader needs to be sensitive to what is happening around them. There may have been a local issue which is on everyone's mind at that moment. Discussing the Ten Commandments may not be what they need at that precise moment.
3. **Individual**
   Never think of a group of people simply as 'a group'. They are a group of individuals, and we need to spot individual needs. It should be easier than in a large group, so should be something we are looking out for.

So, as you lead your small group, be clear about the task you are trying to accomplish (e.g. to learn, understand and apply the story of the Good Samaritan). Around you are a small number of young people who are individuals with needs, at varying stages of maturity, and who are either enjoying the interaction or dreading the moment when they get asked to read or contribute. As you get to know your group, they are getting to know you. Hopefully they'll begin to trust you and your word. You will become an important person in their lives. You never want to create dependence, but to have a leader who they know they can talk to is an important part of youth ministry. In the large youth sessions held at the Keswick Convention, we have two primary aims. The first is to teach the Bible in an age-appropriate way so that God's Word is clear. The second is that every young person attending the convention ends up knowing and being known by one of the leadership team. At the start of our weeks, small groups can be hard work, but they almost always open up by the middle of the week when some very valuable ministry is done. So press on!

Just as you need to be aware of individual needs, so you need to be aware of how the group is working together. There are much more informed sources than me on group dynamics, but be aware of whether there is good interaction. The size of the group matters. In a group of six people (including the leader) there are fifteen relationships (6x5/2). In a group of ten people there are forty-five interactions (10x9/2). Just by increasing the group from six to ten you have tripled the number of relationships, thus magnifying the complexity of the group.

## Starting up

Many people start their group time with an ice-breaker (there are books available) but, whether it is structured or not, it is good to have something which breaks the ice.

Sweets all round can be good, but general chat before the task begins gets the mouth in gear. Apparently it is true that if you say something as unimportant as 'my favourite cereal is Weetabix' your mouth has moved and you are more likely to contribute to more serious matters.

A few starters.

- Make sure your group is sitting in a circle. Set it up so that everybody can see everyone else, because eye contact means non-verbal communication can be seen, as well as verbal better heard.
- Before you start, make sure you've got all you need: Bibles, pens etc.
- If you're going to write down conclusions, either use a flip chart or get a group member to write things down. An alternative is to roll out a large piece of paper in the middle of the group (wallpaper works) and give everybody a felt-tip pen.
- Make sure the group knows how it's going to operate. No put-downs or criticism.
- Be encouraging.

## The questions and the prompts

Getting a group working together can be hard. You put out a question and nobody moves let alone speaks, and you are close to panic. There are various kinds of questions, and your first one should be the easier type. It should be one that is not closed, but is not so broad as to need a doctorate to answer it. We are not trying to be clever in small groups – we are trying to learn about God and his Word together. A few examples of group questions:

- **Closed**

What day is it today? We all know it's Sunday, so why ask.

What's the next verse to Luke 10:7? Probably Luke 10:8.

This gets you precisely nowhere.

- **Factual**

If you've been looking at the Good Samaritan (Luke 10:25–37), you might want to check that the group have understood the story. Make it a sort of general contribution (anybody can answer) time.

Where was the man going?
Who was the first to walk past?
The second?
Where did the Samaritan take him?
What instructions did he leave?

And finish off with: Why was it so significant that the Samaritan stopped?

In asking that last question, you have increased the intensity of the question because you have asked them to make a judgement on why Jesus gave the Samaritan the role he did. You have moved to the

- **Imperative**

'Try to explain the differences between the way that the priest and the Levite acted and how the Samaritan responded' is a question which might prompt a variety of answers. Your job as the leader is to get the group talking about those answers that lead you to what the Bible says.

- Open

These questions are intended to provoke more serious thought and maximize participation. They will normally open with one of the words 'where', 'when', 'why', or 'how'.

'How should we act when we see someone in serious need?' 'Have you ever encountered that at school or college?'

The kind of questions which should be avoided are

- Rhetorical

These require no answer, and the group knows the leader will answer the question anyway.

- Leading

This is where the answer is implied in the question – the question is loaded.

'Can it ever be right to leave some poor beaten up bloke beside the road and do absolutely nothing about it – could you do that?'

- The Vast

'Can you think of all the places in the Old Testament where someone does something similar?' That would take me a couple of hours in the study. For young people, that type of question makes them look ignorant – which is the last thing you want in a group. It's also a 'clever' question, and that's not the objective. It may be better to say, 'Can you think of another character that helped someone in need?'

Questions should be constructed carefully. Here's a set of questions on the Good Samaritan. They are based on Luke 10:25–36.

1. Why do you think a lawyer wanted to test Jesus? (v. 25)

2. Do you think he really wanted to know about inheriting eternal life, or was he trying to catch Jesus out?
3. Why do you think Jesus pointed the lawyer to the Law? (v. 26)
4. The lawyer clearly knew the Law. Wasn't that enough? Why did Jesus have to tell the story? (v. 29)
5. What should have been the response of the priest and the Levite? Why?
6. Why was it significant that it was a Samaritan who helped?
7. What is Jesus conclusion about a 'true neighbour'? What does that suggest to you about who we should help in our daily lives? Don't worry – you can't help everyone you meet who has a need.

Sometimes when you pose the questions you get no response from the group. What do you do then? Do you just sit in silence and wait for someone to speak? Do you just grin at the group in the hope that your lovely smile may prompt a reaction? In preparing your questions, you may find it helpful to have a series of prompts that mean you have something else to say other than just repeating the question. Take question 5 above. I will add some possible prompts which may help young people understand the question, and feel they have something to say.

**Main Question**
'What should have been the response of the priest and the Levite? Why?'

**Prompts**
Any idea what a priest did? Where did he work?
Any idea what a Levite did? (Tell them if they don't know.)

> Do you have a bit of sympathy for them? After all, the man must have looked a bit bloody and messy.
> I think I might have walked by – it keeps life a bit simpler if you don't get involved.

All of those prompts are designed to help the group deal with the original question. Why didn't the two important Jews stop and help? The prompts just talk around that part of the story and give the young people a chance to think of a good response. When you prepare your group time, it's good to have a few prompts ready for all the questions you are going to pose. You may find that with these the group flows more smoothly, but don't be afraid of silence. Sometimes a period of quiet is good for thinking, provided it doesn't become embarrassingly quiet.

## Concluding

One of the hardest things to do with a small group is finish. At the end of a small-group Bible study, it is important to summarize. Your discussion should always be guided by the learning objective, so you need to steer the group towards an understanding of the passage you are looking at. As you draw to a close, bring some sort conclusion using the main point of the application of the story. This means that, as the group breaks up, it feels both that they have contributed and that they have better understood the passage. We are not aiming to establish that all opinions are equally valid, because they're not. God's Word has always been interpreted by commentators down the centuries, but your group time is designed to come to some conclusions and applications which can be followed up by the young people as they try to live their Christian lives. You are certainly not aiming to establish who the cleverest member of the group is. You are using another means of helping young people understand the Bible.

## The challenging ones

There may be some young people who do not respond well to the group situation. Here are some examples and some ways of dealing with them. There may be those who chatter too much, or even try to dominate the conversation. They are always the first to speak and maybe not to the point. At the other extreme, there might be someone who says nothing and may need to be asked to speak. But be careful, their silence may be their choice and they are happy about that. You can get young people who are negative about what has been taught, and those who always seem to be off the subject. Perhaps the hardest to deal with is the joker who thinks everything that is said is worthy of a wisecrack. It is possible to deal with these problems in a group setting – for example, the chatterer can be thanked for their contribution and then asked to let others have an opportunity to speak. But most of these difficulties are best tackled outside the group situation where credibility need not be lost.

**THINK AND ACT**

- Choose a passage of Scripture (maybe one you will soon be teaching).
- At one of the team meetings, spend thirty minutes drafting questions and prompts for the

group time. Each person may like to write two questions.

- Then work on those questions together, and decide which order you will deal with them.
- You can also decide where in the programme the group time is going to happen.

Small groups can be both the most rewarding and frustrating parts of the programme. If they don't go well, it's very easy to feel you've failed. On the other hand, you may experience a real joy in learning something with a group of young people that will encourage them to dig deeper. Because young people feel part of a group, they will want to come back for more, and so small groups lead to larger youth groups. That has to be *good news*.

# BROADER ISSUES

12.

# The Role of the Church

## God's way for his people

If we believe what we read in the press, or accept the popular image, the church has had it. It is seen as a sad anachronism with ancient buildings in inaccessible places, and only populated by those drawing their pension. You only go near the place when you are forced to by attending a wedding or a funeral. When you hear people like Bill Hybels saying 'the local church is the hope for the world',[1] it is hard to believe. Anyway, it's all right for him, he gets 30,000 every weekend to Willow Creek Community Church, and his staff numbers are well into three figures. No wonder he thinks it's the hope for the world. But the Bible does see it that way, and we are trying to do biblical youth ministry

> And he put all things under his feet and gave him as head over all things to the church, which is his body, the fullness of him who fills all in all.
>
> (Eph. 1:22,23)

Christ is not only exalted over all creation, he is the head over all the church. He is its supreme authority and he so identifies with it that he calls it a body – his body! Nothing could be more intimate, and it forces us to the view that the church is about the people and not about preserving tradition or architecture. Churches have traditions, and they can be good and provide a local congregation with security but, if that is what we depend on, no wonder church numbers are dwindling. In every generation, the church needs to rediscover its call and purpose and, if that is solely to run a maintenance operation for an elderly congregation, then it has lost its way. Let us not fool ourselves. It is simply unrealistic for such a congregation to long for hoards of young people to sit in their pews because they fear that in twenty years' time their church will be no more. There has to be a positive reason for joining a church. Children must be warmly welcomed as part of that community, and provision made to teach and train them. There is some debate about how that should happen. Some would argue that children should attend the main services of the church and their parents should continue that process in their own homes. In other words, we don't need a youth group.

I find this view hard to understand. If adult language is being used in adult church, we have to ask what would be the best way for children to be incorporated into that community. As children grow up, their attention span and their use of language improve so, bit by bit, they are more able to understand what is going on. If we want to keep them involved in the community, they certainly need to be included in the all-age church community. But they also need teaching and fellowship with people of their own age, and to be taught in a way they can understand. It is often true that we underestimate children's ability to learn, but I remain unconvinced that a 3-year-old can understand even a small fraction of what is happening in most church services. The child is better served by being given 'spiritual food' they can digest. Our central aim has to be the integration of our children and young people into the full fellowship of the church, but we must ask how that is best achieved.

The term which the early church used to describe itself was *Ekklesia,* which Tyndale translated as 'congregation' – the Authorized Version used 'church'. First-century Greeks used the word to describe any large gathering (Acts 19:32), and Christians used it to describe theirs. They were 'God's crowd' or 'God's called', but the word continued to be used to describe secular gatherings or meetings for the worship of other gods. They didn't want to stick out in society in any way other than that they were God's crowd called by him, saved by him, blessed by him, and loved by him. Nothing's changed. Even though we have seen the church pass through periods of deep division and pain, and periods where it was anything but Christ-like in its behaviour, it remains God's one and only way of his people gathering together.

People who are 'called out' in the Bible are always those who have been delivered from some kind of bondage. In the Old Testament, God's people were delivered from Egypt and Babylon, and we are only Christ's people because he has delivered us from sin and death ('the dominion of darkness' Col. 1:13, NIV). We are called to be in the 'fellowship of his son' (1 Cor. 1:9) just as Israel was called to be in covenant relationship with the God who had delivered them from bondage. We have been called to a future inheritance to be with Christ for ever (Col. 1:12), just as God's people were promised a land flowing with milk and honey. We are called to be his special people, just as Abraham (Gen. 12:2) and Moses (Exod. 3:17) received promises that God would make a great nation. We are God's people called to be in the community of which Christ is the head – we mess with it at our peril.

Yet, as we have seen, children and young people are walking away from the church in large numbers, but the Bible is clear that children have a place in the worshipping community. Children were at the table of the Passover (Exod. 12:26) and Jesus made his attitude to children very clear (Luke 18:16).

I think the phrase that has annoyed me more than any other over the years is when people describe children as the 'church of tomorrow'. This implies that children are adults waiting to happen, and we just long for the day when they will grow up and behave in ways that suit us. The Church of England published a report some years ago which was entitled 'Children in the

Way'. Its doubled-edged meaning neatly conveys the two ways we can think of children.

**THINK AND ACT**

- Which meaning of 'Children in the Way' best describes your church?
- Think of specific ways in which this is true, and what you could do about it.

## Children are a blessing

Men and women come to our churches. They fall in love, get married, and often have children. The Bible is clear that one of the good reasons for marriage is the procreation of children who will need to be loved and nurtured within the community of faith. Whatever you believe about the status of children in the kingdom, it is clearly our duty and our joy to give children the best possible experience of church in their formative years. The church should be a blessing to children, and children should be seen as a blessing to the church. Many people would be happy to turn up to a service of infant baptism and see it as a wonderfully joyful occasion (and so it should be), but miss the fact that promises are made that this baby will be nurtured by that body of believers so that they can truly walk in the way of Christ. Those promises are too easily forgotten as other seemingly more important issues crowd into the life of the child. Playing cricket, writing good stories and acting in school productions are all great things to be part of, and develop a well-rounded child, but they are not what the church has been called to do. We are told to

> Train up a child in the way he should go;
> even when he is old he will not depart from it.
> (Prov. 22:6)

It is our responsibility to make sure our church is an environment where that can happen, and that is the responsibility of *all*, whether we have our own children or not. The whole congregation create that environment, and I am not saying that every service should be an all-age one with large slices of content geared to children, but church should be a place where children feel comfortable and thrive. They are not just to be tolerated, because we have a unique opportunity, in a culture which is fragmented by age divisions, to show that an all-age community can function healthily. I knew of one church where some people deliberately arrived after the children left for their groups, because they couldn't bear the noise of children in the 'sanctuary'. One of the joys in my present church is to see large numbers of children who enjoy the first part of our service and then leave for their session. In my view it is vital that the whole congregation rejoices in the presence of children, and does everything possible to support Christian families.

## Planned provision

Baptisms and dedications (whatever your tradition) are occasions rightly celebrated in our church life. But that little baby will be one year older in a year from that service, and a year older a year after that. Incredibly obvious, maybe, but what is not always appreciated is that that child will need a group or class to belong to for the next eighteen years at least. The birth of a child begins a process of growth and development in which it is the church's responsibility to play its part. Of course, the parents have the key responsibility to bring up their child and nurture them towards personal faith. But part of that process is to provide a community which helps the child on its spiritual journey.

Once that child is born it will need a crèche where it will be secure and enjoy being a part of – that needs leaders, toys and a stimulating environment. Crèche is not a place where we dump children who make too much noise. It is a place where our youngest children enjoy a great time, and are well cared for and stimulated. Impressions are formed at this age and, if they are positive, the young child will get the idea that church is a good place to be.

It is not hard to see that the birth of that child has created the need for groups of all ages to follow on after that. Each group needs men and women committed to a careful and loving ministry of teaching and nurture which is attractive. Some churches struggle to cover the whole age range (only 50 per cent of UK churches have anything for 11 to 18s). This sometimes leads to one church in a particular area becoming 'the place to go' for young people. They love to gather in groups which have a critical mass, so they will generally gravitate towards the larger churches that have the resources to sustain a thriving youth ministry. This creates a scenario which some are uncomfortable with. The family do not all attend the same church. The choices are that the teenager remains at the family's church and worships in the adult service, or moves down the road to the larger youth group. But the ironic thing is that this movement of young people towards larger churches exacerbates the problem in the smaller churches because the young people have now moved out. Perhaps we have been influenced by the culture which suggests that it is all about large numbers. We need a strategy which makes youth ministry effective in a group of four as well as in a group of forty. Some cities have experimented with a both/and strategy. They very strongly encourage young people to stay in their own church for their own group, but supplement it with a city or county-wide meeting twice a term (or however often is useful).

Whatever the size of your group, youth ministry needs to be seen as a significant part of the life of *every church*. The church needs to have youth on its agenda. If there are many under-19s around the place, that ministry needs resources of every kind. In some churches, youth ministry is sustained from the personal finances of its leaders where, at the same time, the church is spending thousands of pounds on building projects. Good work needs materials, rooms as good as you can make them, training for the leaders and, above all, regular and sustained prayer for both the leaders and the children. When the church meets for prayer, pray for the children and young people. In your weekly service sheet, have some news of what's happening with your activities. When the PCC (or other governing body) meets to discuss the business of the church, youth and children should be a regular item on the agenda. In my role as the co-ordinator for youth and children, I regarded the task of keeping the work in the forefront of the life of the church as a key part of the job.

**THINK AND ACT**

- Is youth and children's ministry at the forefront of your church's life?

- How could things be improved? Do you need a press officer? (Doesn't have to be a serving teacher or leader).
- Is your ministry well resourced? What would improve that situation?

If you are to be better resourced, there are ways and means of going about it. I knew a youth leader who, in a blinding flash of inspiration, wanted to improve the look of the rooms they were using. He approached the church treasurer (without warning) and demanded data projectors, screens and laptops in every room because God had told him this was the way to go. The implication was that the treasurer hadn't had the same blinding flash and his cautious response implied, in the mind of the youth leader, a lesser spirituality. In asking the youth minister for a detailed breakdown of cost, the best available prices and the timescale over which these improvements were to be carried out, he had been quenching the work of the Spirit. The treasurer was fulfilling his ministry in being a careful steward of church resources. It's often good if you want something done to approach the appropriate person with your 'possible plan', and then offer to put it in writing with the required details. Incidentally, the youth leader then put about the rumour that the church was not supportive of his ministry. Churches have to deal with many things that take place in their community. Youth ministry is an important one, but not the only one. A responsible request, well documented, is far more likely to be well received than a surprise which is going to cost £10,000.

## Church apart?

In recent years there has been a growing trend to separate the work we do with young people from the main body of the church community. We have seen some youth churches spring up with a greater or lesser degree of separation from an adult congregation, and I can understand the frustration that some leaders have felt as their churches have failed to deal with the concept of multi-generational church. But the youth church is no answer. It is making the statement that church is a single-generation body with no relationships across the ages, and rules out the possibility of Psalm 78 ever operating. How can we tell the next generation the 'glorious deeds of the LORD' if the next generation is now meeting at a different time and in a different place? Despite the frustrations, we have to work this one out because that is how God's Word has designed community for us.

There are children in the church, people get married in church, people retire in church, and people die in a church community. As a pastor you get to see all those things happening in the lives of church families. Children come to a funeral thanksgiving service to say goodbye to their granny, and they confront death and how we understand death as Christians – there is hope beyond the grave and it is good for children to hear that. We will have to learn to get along a little better than at present if Jane and Peter and their children (from chapter 1) are going to find their place – they *all* need to feel that they belong.

We can all caricature the divisions of churches. Old ladies who don't like the drums played too loudly; people who stay away from all-age worship because they find it too trivial, and so on. But the community of faith as expressed in the local church should be the most exciting expression of what God is doing in his world. It is full of people whom God has spoken to and changed, but in some cases the new image has slipped a bit. Here, I believe, is the answer to Jane's dilemma. Once she decided to let her son play sport on Sunday, the pull of the church community on her son should be so strong that his natural inclination is to long to be back with all his mates in Pathfinders (or whatever you call it) because it is there that his strongest peer group operates, and where he hears things about being a Christian runner and student.

To put it simply, the church is a community where you feel you belong and where you hear things that make a lasting impact on your life, and where you can invite your running mates because the cringe factor is low. We cannot throw the concept of the church out of the window when we look at youth work. We have to look at how we do things and see if we could have a framework in place that enables us to grow mature young people into biblical followers of Christ. Jesus' command was to do just that – to 'make disciples' because it's only committed disciples who will be the committed teachers and leaders of the next generation.

## Dealing with parents

One of the pressures often experienced by youth ministers is parents. Children belong to parents – they are primarily responsible for the spiritual growth of their offspring. I once heard Sue Miller (ex head of Children's Ministry at Willow Creek) say that 'what children get here is the icing on the cake'.[2] Many parents struggle with the spiritual aspect of family life. If they are first-generation believers (their parents were not believers) they have no personal experience of living in a Christian home. They struggle with how that differs from perfectly good and loving homes where God doesn't get a mention. I believe this is a major issue for the church of today. Parents *need help*. Most of them make it up as they go along, and often look back with deep regret at the decisions and the guidance they gave. All of us who are parents have moments like that which could have been avoided if someone had given us some help.

For me, getting married was a great experience and one which changed my life for the next forty-three years (and counting). But that change was nothing compared to the arrival of our first child. John-Paul, Mark and Andrew have been wonderful sons (we are so blessed by them, their wives and our grandchildren), but when they arrived they changed our lives – *big-time*. My wife comes from a large Christian family who love the Lord and who understood how to nurture children in Christian ways. I came from a nominal church background where personal discipleship wasn't an issue – we just went to church because we always had. I didn't have a clue how to train my children to be young men with a personal faith in Jesus. I picked that up bit by bit, but nobody taught me how to do it.

I know many parents who struggle with these issues and who either become over-legalistic and imprison their children in a kind of cocoon, or allow them too much freedom. The first type desperately try to shut out the wicked world that surrounds their children, in the hope they won't become infected. When such children leave home, they find a new world which is attractive to them and indulge in it, much to the grief of their parents. The second type allow their children to taste anything without giving them any kind of values or structure. They are allowed to make their own decisions, and often make wrong ones. In my research for my next book about 'the prodigals' (see Appendix 3) I have encountered both types.

There are parents whose primary aim is to keep their children attending church. They want their offspring to be entertained so they will keep coming, and they blame you for their non-attendance because 'you do boring things'. This kind of pressure comes from parents who may be struggling to nurture their child and think that 'church does the spiritual bit'.

My first response would be to say that I hope Bible studies aren't boring. But we must not allow that kind of pressure to deflect us from our primary purpose. Of course we want to make our sessions good to be part of, but teaching people about God is what we are about. It is sometimes helpful to talk to the young person about why they don't like coming. If you dig deep enough, you often find a heart that needs assistance – a good one-to-one may help.

If the only spiritual input teenagers are getting is for one hour in a youth group, then something is wrong. I have spoken to some who say that although their parents are churchgoers, they rarely engage in any kind of conversation with their children about God. They don't know how to pray or read with them. This is one of the main reasons why young people leave the church, and we need to help parents with how to nurture their children. There has to be a consistent Christian voice coming from home and church. Along with parents' training, we need to communicate with them about what we are doing and why. Send them a letter with an outline of your term's teaching programme. Involve them in helping you resource the work – most of them have cars. They are the parents of the children you care for a very small fraction of the week. Whatever you do, don't regard them as the competition. You are working in partnership with the people whom God says are responsible for them – and not just to get them to ballet classes on time.

**THINK AND ACT**

- Think about the conversations you have had with parents. What are the pressures on them?
- What could your church do in regards to training parents?

The future of the church is in God's hands – it is his church. But we are part of it and some of us are called to leadership roles within it; if young people are to mature they must be convinced they are also part of Christ's body.

## Books

John Stott, *The Living Church* (Nottingham: IVP, 2007).
Tedd Tripp, *Shepherding a Child's Heart* (PA: Shepherd Press, 2001).

13.

# Structures That Work

I once worked with a man who delighted in telling me we really didn't need to make plans as God would tell us (him) when he was ready. If you claim to have the only hot line to God in the church we all have to wait for what you decide, and we are powerless to act without your say-so. In the end it leads to the stifling of good initiatives because only the leader can direct, and he becomes the only motivator. If he has a bad day, we all do. We all believe God guides us in the way we do church, but he guides us *together* and that involves some element of strategy and planning. If there is some attempt at planning, the whole place can operate even if the leader gets flu and is off for the week. Corporate planning is not ungodly – quite the reverse.

As I have said before, if you aim at nothing, you'll probably hit it. Of course no plan is cast in stone and may well have to be adapted as situations change – we must not resist those movements of change. That is not a recipe for dogged adherence to a plan written five years ago. If it needs to be adapted then do it, but makes sure everyone knows about the changes. Jesus planned the disciples' mission trips. Paul planned his journeys and did careful research when going to new cities like Athens (Acts 17:22ff.), and I cannot believe Moses didn't do any planning in moving a nation from Egypt to Canaan. It took his father-in-law Jethro to tell Moses, 'You are not able to do it alone' (Exod. 18:18), and if Moses was to share his responsibilities with others in leading God's people in the desert, there had to be clarity about who did what and when, or else the nation would be a shambles. Perhaps 'plans' got a bad press after Baldric's 'cunning plans' in *Blackadder* which were clearly flights of fancy and likely to achieve nothing. I have been in churches where any kind of plan was needed because the church resembled the state of the nation at the end of Judges – 'everyone did what was right in his own eyes' (Judg. 21:25).

Youth ministry is not exempt from the need for clarity of vision and purpose. It should not be done at the last minute because that is spontaneous and that's what young people love. Have you ever stood in a baptismal service (or dedication) as the service leader asks God's blessing on this totally dependent human being that is in his arms, and asked yourself what you want most of all to happen to this child? If you're a parent, you will have asked it about your own children. Of course you long for them to be happy and fulfilled, but the greatest longing for them is that they will follow the Lord Jesus all their days. I think that's what we want for that baptismal baby. That means we must look at how the child will progress through their childhood and adolescence, ending up as an 18-year-old with an appropriate maturity and set-up to move into adult life as a child of God. That means we must plan our work with 0s to 18s to create as few hurdles to vault as possible. We cannot allow our Sunday school to remain separate from our Pathfinders, or Pathfinders from the youth group. They are part of one whole ministry.

If we have only six children from 0 to 11, and we have seen them through Sunday school and we have not prepared what we will do with them at 11, then, with no plan, we will fail. There are many ways of creating a strategy but it is good to have something which describes what you are trying to do. I often used

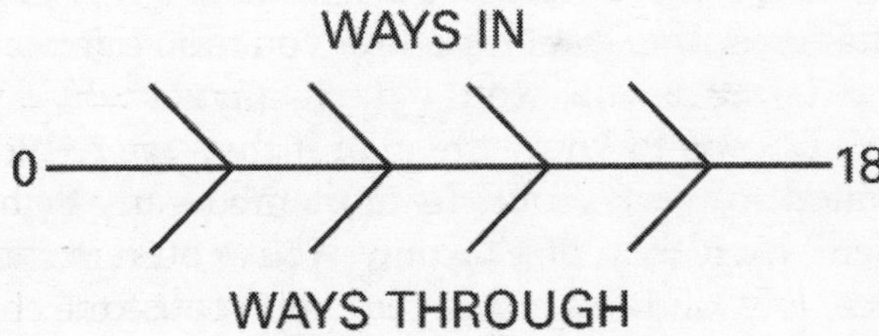


that had a diagram which was a cross between a fishbone and a British Rail sign. It spoke of the need for any child to go through our church and grow as a Christian and not be lost (Ways through). We would do all we could to help that child grow, but we also wanted other children and young people to join us (Ways in) and we would always welcome them gladly. It was just a short phrase, but it gave us a way of remembering what we were doing.

Some people are threatened by the word 'strategy'. They will never be in supreme command of anything, so why do they need a strategy? In the days before the great battle of Alamein in 1942, General Montgomery had many meetings with his generals so that they were all clear about what to do and when to do it. The generals passed all that information to their troops so that when the guns started firing everybody knew their role. Montgomery didn't stop there. He spent hours driving around his troops in their positions and told them exactly what their roles would be when the battle started. His men were willing to fight like tigers because they knew what they were doing and why they were doing it. It shifts motivation from extrinsic to intrinsic. The first way is when you do things only because the leader has psyched you up to do what he says and, as long as you can see him, you keep going, but the leader is the only motivator. When your motivation is intrinsic it is within you. You know what the plan is and you're excited about it. You are as passionate about what you are doing as the leader is. But you don't need him around because you would do it anyway. Everyone involved needs to know the plan if they are to be self-motivated to work it out. Team members begin to feel isolated when they don't know what you're trying to achieve. It is no good just saying you want to do youth ministry because you love working with young people. That's a great start but you need to know how that is to be achieved. Under the guidance of God's Holy Spirit, you seek God's purposes and work them out together. For that you need a plan.

It is easy to make strategic planning sound too grand. It is simply the way one church or youth group plans to go about serving God and their community. It will depend on values and traditions that already exist.

**THINK AND ACT**

- What are the values and traditions that exist in your group, whether it is a church or a youth group.
- At your next leaders' meeting, get every team member to write down what they think the key values are and then compare notes – the results may surprise you.

There is biblical precedent for this – if we follow Paul on his journeys in the Acts of the Apostles, we see that he visited many towns and cities. When he visited Athens he knew much about their temple worship, their culture and their values, which is what made his Areopagus speech so powerful (Acts 17:22ff.). He didn't use his Athens strategy in other towns, but it worked in Athens because he looked at that situation and knew the best way to proceed in that context. A good strategy looks at the place you work in and, based on biblical principles, carries out ministry in a relevant way. Once you have your plan, write it down but don't make it too posh a document because that makes people feel that this is the strategy for the next ten years, and you may have to change your plans in the light of new circumstances.

When we come to our youth and children's work, we often see it through adult eyes. We see that John is doing the fifteen to eighteens and Clive and Dorothy are safe doing eleven to fourteens because they've done it for years. Marie runs sevens to elevens, but we need someone to run fours to sixes because that's done by people once a month on a rota. Crèche is fine because Joan will always be there until the Lord returns. We are looking at our ministry from the point of view of the leaders who run the various groups and, as long as someone turns up each week, all will be well. When I run Root 66 training courses (see Appendix 2) I persuade leaders to draw a picture of their ministry. What I so often see is

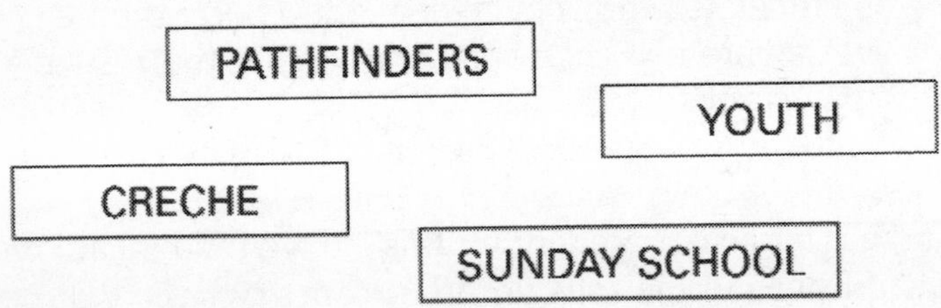


Nothing is connected because they are not seeing their work as the child sees it, moving from one group to another – the 'way through' is not planned, and we just hope they make it. We will look at some of the issues which should help you formulate your own strategy. (I cannot write one for you, because I don't know your situation but hopefully I can give you some helpful questions to ask.) This is always done against the huge backdrop of God's sovereignty – it is his work and we are his servants, but we are trying to do the best job with the resources we have

## Present situation

To formulate any kind of plan, you need to know where you are. If you plan to walk to the South Pole, you don't just grab an extra jumper and set off. You need to be totally honest about where you are – this is not dreamland.

It's a reality check and, even if it's bit painful, it has to be done. It will enable you to decide what the next stage should be. These may be questions you could deal with in your own leaders' meetings or at a leaders' retreat (very useful for this kind of exercise!).

1. Look at your young people.
   Where are they in their own spiritual growth?
   What are their needs?
   Where do they see their future?
   What are the issues that dominate their lives?
   Are there any issues which apply in your area (e.g. high unemployment)?

   It's always good to start with people – understanding your own group is important. They all need the same gospel but, if we are to minister effectively, we need to know about them. Highlighting the issues may lead you to think about teaching certain things, engaging in projects, using different material. Never operate entirely on the principle of 'felt needs', but don't ignore them.

2. Look at your team.
   What gifts do you have in the team?
   What are the roles that need to be filled, and who are the best people to fill them?
   What additional staff are you therefore praying for? (So often we just pray for more team members. If you need an administrator or a caterer, then pray for one – God does understand.)

3. Look at your rooms and resources.
   What kind of room do you meet in – is it the best room you could use, or is there somewhere better? There

may not be, so look at ways you could improve your present environment. Do you have enough Bibles, and could you do with something to make your talks more visual (laptop plus projector may be good; there are some cheap projectors about)?

## Your values

You may never have written down your values, but you have some. There are criteria which you feel passionately about, but those things may not be shared by the whole team. If team members all have different sets of values, you are heading for disaster as soon as something goes wrong. Values act as filters for all the plans and decisions you make, and give a team cohesion and a sense of common purpose. They also determine behaviour – have you ever heard yourself say, 'We just don't do that kind of thing around here.' I'll give you some examples, but don't just copy them, even though I've pinched some of these from churches I know. Your values might be different.

- At all our meetings the Bible will be taught, however briefly.
- We value every individual who comes to our group, whatever their background – we show 'no partiality'.
- We want the group to grow through people becoming Christians, not just because they change churches.
- Everything we do is designed to help young people grow as Christians.
- We want to create a meeting which is the best hour of a young person's week.
- We want to have fun and excitement in our group.

And so on . . .

**THINK AND ACT**

- Have each member of your team (even if it's only two of you) write down the values which are at the heart of your ministry – don't confer at this stage.
- Once each person has written them down, decide which values are non-negotiable for all of you.
- Make sure the whole team has a copy.

By this stage you now know where you are in terms of your group and your resources, and you also know what is important to you.

## First steps

This can sometimes be the difficult bit – the group seems to be ticking along, so why change anything? If you mean that the teaching programme is going well, young people are becoming Christians and being discipled and integrated into the life of the church, then you may be right. When I attended one of Peter Brierley's excellent day courses on the management of change he stated that change is a function of three things

- Malcontent
- Vision
- First steps[1]

I have found these three criteria so helpful over the years because Peter's words are well chosen. Discontent is what you can well do without. Team members on a permanent moaning trip are best ignored as they are probably moaning because they've had a lot of practice and need to shape up. Malcontent is different. It's when you get that niggle inside you that says you're doing all right but you could do this better, and you want to find out how. Bo Boshers, formerly in charge of youth ministry at Willow Creek Church, had a great way of saying this, as I have mentioned before

***Dream your dreams but do your job.***

He is saying the week-by-week ministry needs to keep going, but you need to step back and ask yourself where you are heading. In short, you need a vision, and that is not as grand as it sounds. I've heard some crazy ones in my time, such as the schools worker who was convinced that every student in the local comprehensive school would become a Christian and he would see it happen in the next few months. Unreality like that can lead to terrible disappointment. Much more realistic is a vision that there would be some students, through assemblies and lessons, who would become Christians. And the first step you would take would be to ring the head of RE and offer to take one assembly in the coming term. If that went well you would be invited back, and you could be asked to come twice a term for the next year. You have your vision and the first steps are promising.

## Formulating your strategy

Youth ministers need to learn a vital lesson. What they are doing is not an isolated activity, because it is part of what the local church should be about. What you are doing needs to be communicated to the rest of the church and to your own leaders. Here are some things which will help you to be clear.

- A statement of purpose for your ministry
  We aim provide a group in which we teach God's Word and care for the young people in such a way that they will become more mature in Christ and lead others to him.
  That's probably a bit too long, but better to be clear about your purpose than to be slick and say nothing.
- State your values.
- Decide how your work is to be structured.
  What are the age groups?
  What are the meetings, and what is their purpose (people can then see if your meetings are working out your statement of purpose)?
  Who are the leaders of the groups, and what is their role, if they have a specific one?
- How do all the groups fit together?
  How do children move from one group to another, and what steps are taken if young people stop coming?
- How is the youth ministry related to the rest of the church?

**THINK AND ACT**

- Try writing a strategy document for your youth group. Don't feel bound by my headings – there may be other things which are important to you. If so, write them down.

Although this book is primarily about youth ministry in the local church, I want to briefly broaden its scope. A church's strategy for the under-19s needs to encompass all aspects of the work, from the crèche to older youth. It is painful to watch groups working in isolation caring little about what is happening to the age group below them or above them. It has been said that we lose children in the *gaps* not in the *groups*, so transition from one group to another must be handled with the utmost care. If you are a group leader you must never be just the king of your castle, but you must be very aware and concerned about what is happening in the castles either side of you. How the children are passed from one group to another must be done with loving attention to detail. I once heard a Sunday school leader boasting about the fact that she had held on to the children when they were with her, but what a shame the Pathfinders couldn't keep hold of them! I wonder how many times those two leaders met to plan how those children would move. Did the Sunday school leader invite the Pathfinder leader to visit her group so they could get to know the children moving up? Your strategy should cover everything you do, and the whole work with under-19s seen as a coherent whole.

You may be in a position where you can't deliver a way through. You simply don't have enough people to staff groups at every age. I have sympathy with this because sometimes it is difficult to see what you do with those two children once they reach the age of 11. My plea would be to see this problem from the child's perspective. You can see the problem coming, but you feel impotent. There is nobody in your church who can do this job. I can only suggest three alternatives, but you can always use a combination of these three.

1. When the oldest child in your Sunday school is 9, begin a prayer meeting of parents about what should be done in two years' time. Pray that God will send someone (or someone will emerge) who can do this job. Make it a matter of intercession in the church. Don't leave it until July of the year that child goes to secondary school.
2. Ask your church leaders to identify two people who can lead an 11s to 14s group. Find those people a support group, and make sure they are given adequate resources for their task.
3. Begin talking to another local church and ask them if they can accommodate your 11-year-olds. I would only do this if all else fails but if it means that your young people will still be in fellowship with gospel people, it is worth it. At our church we do have young people whose families go to other churches, but they come to us to attend a youth group they find helpful.

I realize the last point is controversial, but it is increasingly true that not all churches in the land can provide youth ministry. Parents then have to ask the painful question: Would they prefer their offspring to be attending a church even if it is not *their* church?

Whatever happens, it is vital that the plans you have for your youth group are both formulated and communicated. I have known youth leaders who are far too precious about 'their young people' and don't want to tell anyone what goes on in youth meetings. You are not running a secret society. You are running a *part* of the ministry of the local church, and your church needs to know what you're up to, if for no other reason than they will pray for you. Youth leaders have, sadly, acquired the reputation of being 'last minute Larrys' – in my earlier years I was half-affectionately known as 'the late Mr

Fenton'. I long for the day when youth minsters will be known as those who think clearly about their purpose and communicate that to their church and their teams.

**THINK AND ACT**

This may seem strange but try it.

- Draw a picture (or diagram) of your youth ministry. Make sure it includes all the groups who serve under-19s in your church.
- Where groups make a planned and strategic effort to pass on children from one group to the next, draw an arrow linking these groups.
- Where are there no arrows? Where should they be?
- What can you do about it? Think about where you are losing young people and what could be done about it.

# 14.

# Creating the Dream Team

The USA Olympic basketball team of 1996 was labelled the 'dream team'. It was a collection of highly talented players, and every position in the team had the best player who was available. It is rare if you achieve that in ministry. In chapter 2 we looked at how valuable those who make up your team are in serving the young people. We need a balanced team, but above all, men and women of God committed to his service.

Putting two, six or twenty people in one room does not create a team. Teams are not just a coming together of bodies to form a group – that group of leaders needs clarity about its focus and its way of operating. Once we have recruited, we have a team-building operation which will give us unity of purpose and a passion for doing ministry together.

## Biblical models

You may think that teams are a recent idea formed by those trying to create efficient management structures in business. Long before that, God used his people in team contexts, and sometimes not always with a highly visible leader. Moses was the one who sat in the midst of the people of God in the desert (Exod. 18:13). He sat there all day until Jethro, his father-in law, suggested that Moses was trying to do too much.

> What you are doing is not good. You and the people . . . will certainly wear yourselves out, for the thing is too heavy for you.
>
> (Exod. 18:17,18)

Moses saw the sense in appointing others to the work of leading the people of God, and found some trustworthy men whilst he just dealt with the big cases. He had created a team to teach and interpret 'the statutes of God and his laws' (v. 16). The disciples (they were a team of twelve) were sent out in pairs (Luke 10:1) by Jesus; presumably he felt they would be stronger and more able to do the work if they had each other. Paul told Titus (Titus 1:5) to 'appoint elders' and, whenever that happened, the word 'elders' is used in the plural. The early church was led by teams of elders. Proverbs is full of wise words concerning the way people work together and listen to each other.

> Without counsel plans fail, but with many advisers they succeed.
>
> (Prov. 15:22)

Teams are not a modern invention – they are a biblical model of how to do ministry, and it seems that it is how *God designed us* – to work together for the glory of God. There is no room for the Clint Eastwood-like figure that wandered the west and was only happy working alone. Paul often defined his relationship to his friends in the early church as 'fellow workers' (e.g. Rom. 16:3). If teams have their roots in the Bible, we must make them work in the way the Bible defines, which may not be the same way as the business world runs teams.

## The team dynamic

Every team needs something which drives it. As I write this, English cricketers are preparing to go to Australia to defend the Ashes. They don't have any other goal than their passion to win more matches than the opposition. Our team dynamic is very simple, but not always obvious in youth ministry today. It is the *gospel of Jesus Christ*.

It was William Taylor from St Helen's Bishopsgate in London who once said (at a leadership conference)

> The gospel
> CREATES A TEAM
> BUILDS A TEAM
> DEPLOYS A TEAM[1]

We join teams of fellow gospel people because we are passionate about spreading the gospel. As we see God at work we are encouraged to press on and the team is built up. As the team is built up it dares to think it can do more, and is deployed into new areas of ministry. It is not the fact that John (the church youth minister) approached you over coffee one day and made you feel guilty that you weren't doing anything in the church. The guilt was overwhelming so you said 'yes' even though you hate being with young people. That's how your service may start, but it should soon become something which you know God has called you to do. So it is the dual passion to know *Jesus* and *make him* known that gets us out every Friday or Sunday evening to do the work of the gospel. I can remember many nights when my preference would be my armchair and my favourite TV programme. As Paul says

> through whom we have received grace and apostleship to bring about the obedience of faith for the sake of his name among all the nations, including you . . .
>
> (Rom. 1:5,6)

> we had boldness in our God to declare to you the gospel
>
> (1 Thess. 2:2)

We may love working with young people and have a real gift of relating to them, but our primary purpose must be clear: to see these young people grow up into being men and women of Christ. Team unity and common purpose will save a lot of energy because you are all moving in the same direction.

**THINK AND ACT**

- When your team get together, ask them why they turn up each week.
- Some reasons may be very dutiful (and that's needed), but try to work towards the common purpose that leads and motivates your team.
- Once you've decided what it is, write it down somewhere where you will see it regularly (e.g. on your fridge).

Alongside the dynamic of gospel purpose is something which sounds much more mundane, but is equally vital in teams. You don't hear many sermons on Romans 16 (who wants to expound a list of names?). But there are some words which are repeated over and over again in that list

SERVANT
FELLOW WORKER
HARD WORK

We need people in teams who are servant-hearted and will work hard within the time they have available. There are dangers here. People who give the church hour after hour of service and neglect their own families are *not* what we need. There is balance, and it's good to be clear with all your team members about the hours they can *reasonably* give to ministry. It is not an excuse to get out of the house and domestic responsibility.

## Meeting together

One of the most common complaints I hear from youth minsters is that it is hard to get the team together on a regular basis. There is often a very simple reason for this. The team didn't know when the meeting was until the night before when an email arrived at midnight! I always found it best to put leaders meetings on a fixed day in the month (e.g. first Thursday) because people get in a rhythm of when to come. You will often be working with busy people so it's sensible to get a year's worth of dates in the diary. Leaders meetings should be crucial to the health of the ministry, so need to have some structure and purpose about them. Not every meeting should start with the dreaded line 'Does anyone have anything to raise?' Agendas sound rather businesslike, but they do mean that things get talked about that are the issues of the time.

Meetings have many functions. Broadly speaking, your team meetings should be used for

- Administration
- Organization
- Training
- Prayer
- Fellowship
- Pastoral care

Not every meeting should have all those elements. One evening could be usefully spent going through the names of the people in your group and praying for them one by one. Another evening could be spent organizing the term with all the rotas and duties sorted out in one go. It's also good to spend time going through the passages or book you are going to teach. This is the kind of thing that gets squeezed out because you are still deciding who is doing what next Sunday. Get that done and dusted in one meeting and you have bought the time to study the Bible together. You often find that leaders value the chance to pray with one another – not about youth ministry, but about the issues in their lives. You should not ignore the fact that somebody in your team is about to be made redundant or has an aged parent who lives 200 miles away and needs to be regularly visited. There will always be pressures on members of your team and you can't ignore them – your recognition of them will, in itself, build the team. At the end of a year of working together you will be able to look back on ten or twelve fruitful meetings, and celebrate with a Chinese take-away (I know how to live!).

## Many gifts – one purpose

Every single believer has been given a spiritual gift. God says so.

> To each is given the manifestation of the Spirit for the common good.
>
> (1 Cor. 12:7)

The gifts are given to every believer, not so that they can boast, but for the benefit of others. It is often true that in a team of youth leaders, the gifts of the team are not known. Everybody turns up each week to be with the young people. Everyone tries very hard to get to know them, and then goes home again. But the list of gifts includes teachers, and not everyone is a gifted teacher. The sad thing is that groups often operate on a 'have a go' principle, and we need to be more careful than that. It is far more efficient to discern the gifts of the team, use them in their area of gifting, admire what they do and encourage them.

Here is a simple exercise to assess the contribution of every person in the team. You should use this tool with flexibility, but it may point to some more detailed work you can do in gift assessment.

1. Write down twelve tasks that need to be done to keep your youth ministry going. I have started the list – you need to fill in the rest of the roles which should be specific to your group.
2. Take the twelve activities and give them a rating in the 'enjoyment' column.
   The four you most enjoy doing – score 3
   The four you least enjoy doing – score 1
   The other four tasks – score 2
3. Do the same with 'proficiency' column
   Those you think you are really good at – score 3
   Those you think you are least good at – score 1
   The others – score 2

An example

| **Tasks Roles & Activities** | **Enjoyment** | **Proficiency** | **Contribution E x P** |
|---|---|---|---|
| **1. Leading a small group** | **3** | **2** | **6** |
| **2.** | | | |
| **3.** | | | |

Note: E x P is Enjoyment x Proficiency. Here it is 3 x 2 = 6.

Now complete the whole table

| Tasks Roles & Activities | Enjoyment | Proficiency | Contribution E x P |
|---|---|---|---|
| 1. Teaching the Bible | | | |
| 2. Cooking food | | | |
| 3. Leading small groups | | | |
| 4. Performance drama | | | |
| 5. Leading sung worship | | | |
| 6. Praying for young people | | | |
| 7. | | | |
| 8. | | | |
| 9. | | | |
| 10. | | | |
| 11. | | | |

Generally there are up to four tasks which clearly emerge as the ones you enjoy and, not surprisingly, are in your areas of gifting. This may well help you give members of the team a clear role which they can exercise for the blessing of others. In the Sheffield youth group, we had one lady whose ministry of prayer and pastoral care was the backbone of what we did. She gave many hours to carefully praying through the list of our young people and following up on earlier conversations. She would not have considered herself the greatest teacher in the world. Ideally, every member of your team should have a clear responsibility which is acknowledged and valued by the rest of the team.

However, there are sometimes moments where the work is not about gifting. It is when all members of the team have to get a job done, such as clearing up at the end of the evening. Your teacher does not disappear because washing up the cups is not his gift. A combination of a particular responsibility coupled with a willingness to get stuck in to a communal task is a great way to build the life of team.

## Changing teams

In the chapter on small groups we looked at the number of relationships that exist within a group situation. In a leadership team we need to be very conscious of relationships within a team and how they develop. Failure to do this can lead to all kinds of tension of petty jealousies. Phrases such as 'He gets all the best jobs!' or 'Why does he get more teaching slots than me?' can develop if there has not been good discussion about who does what. At times there may be a need for a clear decision from the leader, but the most lasting decisions are made when these have been agreed rather than forced on the members of the group. One thing that can affect a team is the arrival of a new member. As a simple example take a leadership team of six, where one person has left and another has arrived. In a group of six there are fifteen relationships. With the arrival of a new member there are five new relationships needing to be developed (one third of the total). One person changes the whole dynamic of a team, and you are unwise if you fail to recognize the effect of this new member. If two leave and two arrive in a group of six, ten new relationships out of fifteen are new (two-thirds of *all* relationships are new). That's why, if there are changes to a team, you need to do some team-building exercises to create a good team spirit.

**THINK AND ACT**

- Recall the time when a new person joined your team – did it cause a problem?
- What could you do to help graft in new team members?

## Changing direction

If your team is not working well, you may be wondering if a change of direction is needed. The meetings are not very positive and you don't seem to be making much progress with your ministry. You've reached a dead end, and you're not sure how to get out of it. When you are completely involved with the life of a youth group, it is sometimes hard to see any direction ahead. You seem to lack purpose. What you need is what some have called 'smart goals'. What do they look like?

1. They are specific.
   I once helped a group whose stated goal was to reach every secondary student in the city with the gospel of Christ. Sounds great, but they had fifteen members and the city was a big one. The team of leaders amounted to four.
   They would never see it happen, so could never say 'we've done it'. It was more realistic to say 'a clear understanding of the gospel for all members by Christmas'.

2. They can be measured.
   Starting with a goal of 'one discipleship group of three boys within two months' is something you can look at and say you've done it or you haven't. Then you can either rejoice together or sit down and decide the next goal in the light of your recent experience.
3. They must be 'in range'.
   Does this youth group have the resource to make this happen? Do we have the time, the staff, the resources to achieve what we set out to do? Many good ideas start, but many have not been maintained because they are simply too big for the group.
4. Realistic and able to be reviewed.
   The 'gospel to every student' goal is way out of range. To 'attempt to form a link with one secondary school' is something which you sense might happen. Then you work towards it, you pray about and in God's good time you may well see it happen. Are there places along the way where you can look at how you're progressing and assess whether the project is going well, needs adapting or should be shelved?
5. They should be timed.
   When will this be done by? I once met a team who were planning on decorating the room they used. Ten years later it was still the same rather tatty room which, with a coat of paint, could have been transformed. I didn't dare ask them if it was still in their future plans.

If you think there are specific things wrong with the functioning of your team, you may like to use the following checklist. Don't be afraid of looking at these issues as they help you grow as a team together. This exercise can be well used as part of one of your meetings.

| Possible problems in the team | Never happens | Applies | Always happens |
|---|---|---|---|
| No clearly defined goals | | | |
| Responsibility not given to team members | | | |
| Every week there's a change of plan | | | |
| Gifts not recognized | | | |
| Time expected is too demanding | | | |
| No training | | | |
| Too many e-mails/texts | | | |
| Meetings lack structure | | | |
| Uncertain about the future direction | | | |
| No encouragement within the team | | | |
| No support from the church | | | |
| There's a crisis most weeks | | | |
| We simply don't know what's happening next week | | | |
| Everything's done last-minute | | | |
| We never seem to have time to pray | | | |
| We rarely open our Bibles together | | | |

If we are going to work in teams, we need to recognize that they don't just become good teams without the members making them work. If we are working with others in ministry, we need to be committed to our 'fellow workers' as much as Paul was in Romans 16. Of course we are committed to the young people we minister to but, over the years, I have come to really treasure the teams I have worked in either as their leader or simply as part of the team. Doing gospel ministry together is very powerful.

## EPILOGUE

# Dealing with Joy and Pain

My intention in writing this book is to better equip those who, week after week, serve God faithfully in youth ministry. Whether you're new to it or if you've been doing it for years, nobody pretends it is anything but hard work. Hopefully the hard work is bearing fruit in your group but if it isn't, there are times when we are simply called on to keep going. You are doing the same thing as you did the year before, but everything seems to be going wrong. The young people are not listening to the teaching or participating in small groups, and you are certainly not seeing the fruit in their lives. Turning up week by week can be hard in those circumstances, particularly if you can't see how to put things right.

My hope is that some of what you have read gives you ways to address the problems, coupled with a renewed sense of purpose. One of things that deflates youth ministers is the feeling that you are only doing something because you did it last year and the year before that. If you lack vision you will lack purpose, and your sole motivation will be to keep going and do the things you've always done. My garage door desperately needs a new coat of paint. We keep saying we're going to get it done, but it remains unpainted and drab. There are occasions (not every year) where you take a look at what you are doing and why. This needs prayer and careful planning, coupled with care for your team members, who may be threatened by uncertainty. I have nothing but deep admiration for those who faithfully turn up each week and do the work of ministry. You may never be aware of what has happened in the lives of those who come to your group. In the nicest possible way – you do not have a clue what you are doing.

We have dealt with many issues, but ultimately youth ministry is about dealing with the lives of young people. We get to know them and they become part of our lives. We get to know their strengths and weaknesses. Sometimes there are those who annoy us, and it is awfully possible to develop favourites. But they are all God's children and deserve the best we can do for them in helping them mature into faithful followers of Jesus. That aim should always be at the forefront of what we do – that is our core purpose and we deviate from it at our peril. In any other aspects of their lives, we see young people grow and develop bit by bit from one year to the next. A boy who picks up a tennis racket at 5 and shows some promise would not be a match for Andy Murray on the centre court at Wimbledon. If he is to scale those lofty heights, he needs to be coached and developed through those childhood and teenage years to realize his potential. We need to see all the work we do from 0 to 18 as striving towards maturity in discipleship – in other words *growing up* from a baby Christian when first they come to faith to the time when they face an adult world equipped to keep following Jesus Christ.

We rejoice that many do stick with their walk with God. And we need to learn to be thankful for that. But always be thankful that it is only through the mercy of God that that 18-year-old now has a way of living for Christ in their world. You, as one of their leaders, have had a part in that, and you can give God the glory that that person is leaving for the world of work or college to be someone who will make a difference. That is something to be celebrated and to be thankful about. I sometimes get Christmas letters from former youth group members, and it is great to see how some of them have gone forward. I fondly remember a quieter girl from the youth group who married a Christian man – they have had children and are now part of a youth leadership team in their church. It doesn't get any better than that and it is all right to go to an open space and have a little jump for joy (or something less obvious). Stories of God's grace should be celebrated by the team – you laboured hard for those young people and God loves a celebration (he's got a big one lined up for heaven). However, if ever that becomes group pride, you're in trouble. Always keep in mind the fact that you are a servant of God and *he* has enabled you to do a good job – then you can celebrate what *God* has done.

> But thanks be to God, who in Christ always leads us in triumphal procession, and through us spreads the fragrance of the knowledge of him everywhere.
>
> (2 Cor. 2:14)

The lives we invest in our youth groups have (on average) at least another sixty years to 'spread the fragrance of Christ' around. They may become leaders in Christian Unions at university. Hopefully they will have Christian marriages (if they get married) and have children who they'll bring up to know and love the Lord. They will serve in churches – become the elders, pastors and Sunday school teachers of the future. What we are doing in youth ministry may well determine the whole future life of that young person. As most of them go into the workplace, they become the Christians in the workplace of the future. And many of them will make a difference. If we do not engage in serious youth and children's ministry, none of this future hope will ever happen. It will bring us great joy, but of greater importance will be the growth of God's kingdom.

On the other hand, most of us probably have stories of young people who have come and gone. There will always be the occasional visitor who pops in but doesn't stay. But the greater sadness is the person who is part of the group for many years and then either drifts away or, one day, just doesn't come any more. To suggest this is less than real heartache is to trivialize something very sad. They have been in the same group-times, been on the same house parties, been part of all the same activities as those who have stayed the course but, for some reason, it just doesn't appeal any more. Why this happens is part of my next project (see Appendix 3) but when it happens it is deeply upsetting. People often ask, 'What did we do wrong?' and there is value in asking that question if it results in us looking at what we do and how we could do it better. But there are many factors outside our orbit which may have contributed to the parting. Young people from homes where parents are not Christians sometimes have a hard struggle and give up. Peer pressure can contribute and a bad relationship can exert a strong influence on how the young person feels about the group.

Knowing the reason for their departure can be helpful, but doesn't ease the pain. My only solution to dealing with this pain goes a bit like this

1. Do you all can to keep in contact with them and tell them you miss them.
2. Ask if there is anything they would like to talk about.
3. Send them a text or email about future events (e.g. weekends or house parties).
4. Encourage young people who go to the same school or college to keep the channels open.
5. Pray.
6. If it is a Christian family, it may be helpful to talk to parents.

In all these things we are seeking restoration. We long for that young person to be restored to the group and be taking a full part again. But there may come a time when you've run out of restorative ideas and you have to move on. I often found myself thinking years later about people who had been part of our group. My best experience, which encouraged me never to give up hope, was a girl who had been part of our Pathfinders group and came mostly to the midweek club. Apparently one night I gave a short talk and an illustration was a globule of oil in a glass cube which had been the first oil to hit the shore from the North Sea. About four years later, this girl reappeared at the senior youth group when we did a late-night hike over the Derbyshire hills. After we had been walking a short while, I was conscious of someone walking beside me. It was this girl and she reminded me that I had given a talk the last time she was around, about North Sea oil. To say I was encouraged that she had remembered is an understatement. She soon became absorbed into the group, became a Christian and went on from there.

Not all the stories are good, but we must always remember God calls on us not to be successful but to be faithful. Some do return from the 'far country', but many do not. Having done all we can to restore wanderers, our task is to keep on being faithful in ministry, to do what we can. And it is a beautiful thing (Mark 14:3–9) to, as it were, lay our gifts before God and do what we can as long as the Lord gives us breath.

Youth ministry is a wonderful calling. Let's keep going *until he comes*.

# APPENDICES

# Appendix 1

# Arranging the Food

Getting a one-year plan together can be a struggle. You will remember that the Bible is made up of various genres, and our aim is to give the youth a balance of those, as well as deal with topical issues. You may well come across young people who ask you to deal with certain books or genres. I would respond positively to that but also aim to keep the balance in the programme. It is probably not wise to go for 'themes' rather than books of the Bible. Teaching themes may give us license to teach either our 'favourites' or the particular agendas which we're into at the moment. Each of the boxes in the following examples is anything between four and six sessions long. After that you probably need a change, but in one term you have looked at three different areas.

## Example 1

This is simply an attempt to cover a variety of genres. You could easily replace Joseph with Moses, but it's probably not wise to do the whole of the life of Moses in twelve weeks (the whole of one term). It probably works better if you teach Moses in two halves of six weeks.

| TERM 1 | TERM 2 | TERM 3 |
|---|---|---|
| Five parables in Mark's gospel | 'In the beginning' Genesis 1 – 3 | Joseph in Egypt |
| Psalms to live by The Psalms of Ascent | The early life of David | A chapter to die for Romans 8 |
| Christmas in the prophets, Isaiah, Micah, etc. | Easter in John's Gospel | Changed lives in Acts 1 – 8 |

The next example is one where there are themes and a book returns.

## Example 2

| TERM 1 | TERM 2 | TERM 3 |
|---|---|---|
| Moses – his early life | James – new year resolution | Themes in Proverbs |
| Big Issues – suffering, environment, lifestyles, etc. | Moses – the desert leader of a nation | New life, new churches in Acts |
| Wise men, shepherds and a star! | Isaiah talks of Jesus | Joshua conquers the land |

One of the things young people find it hard to grasp is the big story of the Bible. Books like Vaughan Roberts' *God's Big Picture*[1] are accessible to young people and can be used to help see how it all fits together. This can be used effectively both as a basis for teaching sessions and small-group discipleship settings. Having a framework to fit a book such as Amos into helps them to understand it better. So the third example has a bit of 'Bible overview' feel about it, and is designed to give the group a better understanding of the Bible's story at the end of a year.

## Example 3

| TERM 1 | TERM 2 | TERM 3 |
|---|---|---|
| God's big picture:<br>From creation to the promised land | The seven churches of Revelation | The parables of Jesus |
| The early picture After Adam and up to Abraham | Amos<br>The social conscience of the Old Testament | God's Big Picture:<br>God's plan for the future beings – New Testament |
| Themes in the Bible, Grace or salvation | God's Big Picture:<br>People in land longing for a Saviour | How it all ends<br>Later chapters of Revelation |

None of these examples should be slavishly followed, but I hope the principle is clear. All Scripture is worth teaching – there is nothing off-limits. I have given you plans for one year, but you need to keep an eye on what you do over a longer period. In youth groups you will probably have students with you for three or four years. If you put three or four-year plans together you can cover a lot of Scripture. Planning at this level saves you from teaching the story of Joseph twice and completely ignoring Moses.

One thing I should say at this point is that I am no good at titles (you probably spotted that!). So ignore mine and write some better ones. Most biblical genres have been touched upon, so your young people have been exposed to the rich variety of the Scriptures. Hopefully it will whet their appetites for the whole of the book, not just the nice stories.

# Appendix 2

# Root 66

Route 66 happens to be the name of a big road in America, but it is really a training course for Youth Leaders! It is about biblical youth ministry, so its root is the sixty-six books of the Bible. We run discipleship weekends for young people at the Oakes in Sheffield (info@oakes.org.uk) – please book through the Oakes. There is limited amount of consultation work available to churches who want to review what they are doing with youth ministry. That will either be done by me or one of the many highly competent members of the Keswick Youth team who live close to where the help is needed.

Our main business is running evening/day/half day courses anywhere in the UK. We have a website called Root 66 so you can see all the details of how it works, but a few practical details may help you.

1. The course is designed to meet your local needs. It needs a church in an area to decide that its workforce needs training, and to fix a date. Then they contact us to see if a trainer is available. The courses are run by members of the Keswick youth team who are

based all over the UK, and can come to a church near you.

2. It is best if you then gather together other church youth teams in the area. You may need some simple fliers to advertise the course. You have the local networks, so it's preferable if you do the invitations.
3. The arrangements for the day are up to you, but we have found it best to keep things simple. Offer to provide a constant supply of tea and coffee with biscuits, and encourage people to bring their own lunches.
4. Decide when you want to hold the course – 10 till 3 on a Saturday seems to work quite well, but some have found doing just a morning is preferable.
5. Decide which topics you want to cover in your training – there is a comprehensive list on the website. One topic can occupy the whole day, or we can do two or four topics in a day, depending on the depth you want to go into.

Please get in touch if you would like further information. We hope these courses will act as a follow-up to some of the principles laid down in the book.

Contact dave.fenton1@btinternet.com
or dave@keswickyouth.com

# Appendix 3

# The Prodigals

Over recent years I have become increasingly concerned about the numbers of young people leaving the church. The statistics are obvious from organizations such as Christian Research. There have been some very helpful books published about how the issue is handled pastorally (and that is vital), but we are a bit reluctant to ask the 'Why?' question. Why did he or she leave?

I have done a few interviews with young people who have left church youth groups and I have been quite surprised by the responses. This work is at the early stages and I hope to publish it soon, but I need more interviews. If you know of people who might be willing to talk to me I would be very glad to hear from you. Needless to say, interviews would be conducted in 'proper places' and anonymity would be guaranteed. Please contact me on dave.fenton1@btinternet.com.

If you, as a youth leader, have insights about the issue of prodigals, I would love to include your reflections in the book. It seems slightly strange that we have invested huge sums of money in the British church in funding youth ministry (mainly full- or part-time workers), but still we are leaking young people. Before we invest any more resources, the 'Why?' question is worth asking. At a far deeper level, these young people are often part of Christian families for whom this issue is a massive heartache. They are often riddled with guilt and experiencing real pain as they see their children drift away from the Lord. If we understand why, we may be able to do some mending.

Please get in touch with either names or insights or both.

# ENDNOTES

## Introduction

[1] Actual source unknown; quote heard in a talk given by George Carey at Holy Trinity Brompton twenty years ago.

## 1. The World of Youth Ministry

[1] P. Brierley, *Pulling Out of the Nose* Dive (London: Christian Research 2006).

## 2. Faithful Servants

[1] G. Burton, *People Matter More Than Things* (London: Hodder & Stoughton, 1965).
[2] Said by Bo Boshers on a training course.

## 4. Growing Up: A Place to Become Christians

[1] Heard on a training course.
[2] *Two Ways to Live* (Australia: Matthias Media, 2003).

## 5. A Place to Learn How to Live and Grow as Christians

[1] David Watson, *Discipleship* (London: Hodder & Stoughton, 1983).

## 7. The Role of the Bible

[1] *Pleasure*, published by the Centre for HIV and Sexual Health at NHS Sheffield, 2009.

## 8. The Teacher and Learner

[1] Heard at a training course for Mission England 1985.

## 9. Preparing to Teach

[1] Paraphrase of words spoken in the article 'An unusual approach to a big challenge'; John Martin talks to Peter Ward (*Times Educational Supplement*, 1993).
[2] Phil Moon, *Young People and the Bible* (Grand Rapids, MI: Zondervan, 1993).

## 12. The Role of the Church

[1] Bill Hybels: Leadership Conference at Willow Creek Community Church, 1993.
[2] Quote heard on a training course.

## 13. Structures That Work

[1] Christian Research – Management of Change training course.

## 14. Creating the Dream Team

[1] Heard on a training course at Oak Hill.

## Appendix 1

[1] Vaughan Roberts, *God's Big Picture* (Nottingham: IVP, 2004).

## All One In Christ Jesus

### *A Passionate Appeal for Evangelical Unity*

David Coffey

Jesus prayed that all his disciples would be one . . . and yet we are a long way from that. In fact, it appears that divisions within the evangelical world are hardening, with many of us going to those conferences, listening to those speakers and reading those books and newspapers which will simply confirm us within our tribal divisions – and we are increasingly neglecting our God-given responsibility to seek for unity. David Coffey has worked across the tribes for many years, and in this book he calls on all evangelicals to be prepared to pull down their barriers and to reach out to each other for the sake of reaching this needy nation with the gospel. A church united in truth and mission could be much more fruitful in serving the Lord.

978-1-85078-830-0

## Discipleship

Peter
Maiden

Every Christian is called to be a disciple, but do we realise this? And what does it mean?

Peter Maiden, after a lifetime of discipleship, shows from his own struggles and experiences that the life of discipleship is a life of relationship – a love between us and Jesus. We are called to servanthood, to being wise in the use of time and money. Then there are things we can do to help ourselves: the spiritual disciplines of prayer, Bible study, fasting; and things we can do to help each other as church communities. Finally, he looks at what it is all for – mission – and who it is all for – Jesus.

**978-1-85078-762-4**

978-1-85078-748-8

978-1-85078-579-8

**978-1-85078-881-2**

**978-1-85078-695-5**

**978-1-85078-481-4**

**978-1-85078-643-6**

978-1-85078-749-5